MW01536462

Uncommon Community

Uncommon Community

One Congregation's Work with Prisoners

John Speer

For Gena,

With gratitude for your work and your spirit.

John Speer

SKINNER HOUSE BOOKS
BOSTON

Copyright © 2008 by John Speer. All rights reserved. Published by Skinner House Books, an imprint of the Unitarian Universalist Association of Congregations, a liberal religious organization with more than 1,000 congregations in the U.S. and Canada. 25 Beacon St., Boston, MA 02108–2800.

Printed in the United States

Cover design by Kathryn Sky-Peck
Text design by Suzanne Morgan

ISBN 1-55896-538-6
978-1-55896-538-6

6 5 4 3 2 1
11 10 09 08

Library of Congress Cataloging-in-Publication Data

Speer, John.
    Uncommon community : one congregation's work with prisoners / John Speer.
        p. cm.
    ISBN-13: 978-1-55896-538-6 (pbk. : alk. paper)
    ISBN-10: 1-55896-538-6 (pbk. : alk. paper) 1. Church work with prisoners.
2. Unitarian Universalist Association—Doctrines. 3. Unitarian Universalist
churches—Doctrines. I. Title.

BV4340.S64 2008
259'.509764135—dc22
                                                                2007052315

All writings by prisoners are printed with permission from the authors. "Letters Come to Prison" by Jimmy Santiago Baca was previously published in *Doing Time: 25 Years of Prison Writing*, edited by Bell Gale Chevigny.

This book is dedicated to my beloved friend and collaborator K. Limakatso Kendall. Much of the passion and insight that readers will find here is hers. Because of its infectiousness, I now call it mine as well. Thank you, Kendall, for drawing me into the prisons and for the loving kindness you bring to all those around you.

—John Speer

Note to Reader

Many of the prisoners mentioned in this book are referred to by their first names only. Certain individuals have given explicit permission to use their full name; in those cases, both their first and last names are provided. No aliases are used in this book.

In the terminology of prison life, non-prisoners are referred to as "free-world people." The same term is used here.

Contents

Foreword

WHENEVER I SPEAK AT UU CHURCHES about my work as a prison chaplain, people approach me afterward with stories of family members in prison, friends in the criminal justice system, and even their own time behind bars. This used to surprise me. I thought I was preaching to congregations about reaching out to people who are different from us and bridging the gap. I used noble metaphors of inclusion and transformation, of expanding the number of voices at the table. These metaphors are still noble I am sure, but they take on a different cast when we're talking about ourselves.

The other story I hear a lot is "I don't understand how liberal religion works in a place like that." At first I thought this was a question of beliefs—how does our theology suit us for prison work? That one is easy to answer—we are an inclusive tradition, affirming many experiences of the Holy, and this approach fits well in multi-faith settings like prisons and jails. We have a heritage of Universal Love that manifests itself in acts of caring and compassion. We are committed to social justice and equity in human relations, both sorely needed in the criminal justice system. And we have Principles and Purposes that remind us of our connections with all people and the dignity and worth of every human life.

But I am not so sure these ideas are enough, or that they are even the foundation of our usefulness in this work. What makes a liberal theology effective in prison work is not the answers it gives or the interpretations it imposes on the world. We work with many people who have different understandings and experiences than we do ourselves. So a theology that is worth anything in this setting should be valued by its ability to build relationships, to live with ourselves and with each other in the most fundamental ways possible. Liberal religion works because it calls us into community and inspires us to relate. It works because it wakes us up, reminds us of who we are, and calls us to be with others.

Building relationships is no easy task, however. We are easily lulled into (or scared off by) the romantic notion that relationships are all about harmony and peace, about magical connections and mushy enmeshment. Yet, paradoxically, quality relationships require separateness. They need a space between us that allows for me to be me and you to be you, a space that honors our differences and requires us to build bridges of conversation, mutuality, and care. These bridges are not based on a co-dependent need for happiness and health, but on a nuanced awareness of boundaries and connections that respects our selves, our roles, and our abilities. In fact, these boundaries allow us to reach out beyond ourselves and listen to others' stories. When we are with people in this way we do not become them. We do not live their lives or make their decisions or save them from themselves. We witness. We encourage. We share. We relate. This kind of togetherness is the call of our religious community. And it is the most dynamic, effective, and miraculous gift we can bring.

This book tells the story of how one Unitarian Universalist community built meaningful relationships with prisoners. Through letter writing, writing workshops, and mentoring opportunities, John Speer, K. Limakatso Kendall, and the Henry David Thoreau UU Congregation provided occasions for inmates and outsiders to engage with one another and establish a sense of community. Their work was not always smooth or easy, but it shows an inspiring dedication to create connections with those on the other side of the fence.

The authors are not the only UUs involved in such tasks. The Unitarian Church of Harris, Pennsylvania, partners with the Pennsylvania Prison Society and the Program for Female Offenders in helping women in prison and their families. The Restorative Justice Team at Unity Church-Unitarian in St. Paul, Minnesota, supports its members in a number of activities including mentoring inmates, hosting restorative justice workshops, teaching classes in prison, working with ex-offenders, and more. Atkinson Memorial Church in Oregon City, Oregon, collects children's books, yarn, and other miscellaneous items for the local women's prison, and the UU Fellowship of Central Oregon in Bend collects religious books for the prison chapel library. And the UU Church of the Larger Fellowship sponsors an effective letter-writing ministry between UU inmates and outsiders nationwide.

Individuals across the country are involved as well—tutoring, teaching quilting, holding prayer circles, walking labyrinths, and offering classes that help prisoners explore their spirituality. All of them are connecting, participating in the creative force of relationship, helping others and themselves to live more meaningful lives.

When I began this work, my mentor, Mickey Friesen, often talked about breathing underwater. So often we see people drowning and we want to rescue them, pull them out of the water so they can rest and breathe and start anew. We toss a rescue buoy their way. Usually, though, the rope tangles at our feet, the buoy falls short of our aim, and we're lucky if we don't get pulled in ourselves. Or it hits them on the head and knocks them out cold, making the situation even worse. If we do manage to throw it just right, we pull them out and they catch their breath and rest for awhile. But eventually they will have to get back in. It is their life, after all—their relationships, their histories, their choices and happenings. People have to live their lives.

What if instead of rescuing people we helped them learn to breathe underwater? What if we helped them tap into those little bubbles of air around them—bubbles of hope, faith, strength, or healing? When we help people access the resources around them, we help them to find Life amidst their struggles. So the central act of caring and being in relationship with one another is not about solving problems or saving people. It's about helping people learn how to breathe.

This book is the culmination of many breaths. It is my personal hope that it will encourage others to engage in the mysterious wonder of ministry to prisoners. As we live out our faith and engage the power of our religious community, may we be inspired to live and breathe and share our being with one another in faith, hope, and love. Blessed Be.

—Rev. Dr. Emily Brault

Introduction

THERE ARE EIGHT PRISONS within a fifteen-mile radius of the Henry David Thoreau Unitarian Universalist Congregation in Stafford, Texas, and more than 33,000 prisoners of the state of Texas live within an eighty-five mile radius of our community. We live in a political district where "get tough on crime" rhetoric wins votes, and where candidates for electoral office do not talk about providing opportunities for prisoners to change their lives.

Our church community is called to work with prisoners for personal, political, and spiritual reasons. At least a fourth of our 150 members has provided direct service to prisoners, and many more have been involved in advocacy or indirect service of various kinds. Some of us have family members in jails and prisons. Some are most interested in public education and advocating for policy change. K. Limakatso Kendall (known by friends as Kendall) and I have been the primary facilitators of our congregation's work with prisoners. We are drawn particularly toward direct contact with individuals. We like real letters in envelopes with stamps on them and face-to-face meetings and volunteer workshops held in prison classrooms. We like to touch the lives of specific human beings whose stories we can learn, and who have time to listen to us and help us grow.

This book describes three projects initiated and supported by our congregation involving direct contact with prisoners: a letter-writing program that allows us to foster relationships with prisoners;

a creative-writing workshop in a prison classroom, that spawned a literary journal called *Midnight Special*; and a program for college teachers that allows prisoners to serve anonymously as tutors and writing mentors to college students. In these pages, I describe how we set up these programs, examine some of the mistakes we made in the hope that others will not make the same ones, and discuss how other congregations could start their own programs.

Less practically, but even more important, I discuss how our prison work grows from and contributes to our religious practice. This work is important for our congregation, for Unitarian Universalism, and for the inner lives of those of us engaged in the effort. I focus especially on two concepts: building community and finding freedom.

Community is a group of individuals stumbling toward our better selves with mutual respect. Community requires acts of courage like laughing together at our dumbest mistakes, reliving our losses, admitting our shame, asking hard questions, and accepting each other's praise. As we build community with prisoners across differences of class, race, and background, we are lifted out of our ghettos of privilege or struggle. We meet each other, hear each other's stories, and exclaim, "I never knew anybody like you before." Or, we say, sometimes, "We are so much the same despite our differences." The wonder of revelations like this tickles us into sheepish grins and then rips our hearts open.

Healthy communities of trust, support, and mutual respect nurture and encourage good decision making. These assets are glaringly absent from prison life. Creating relationships with prisoners improves the likelihood that they will grow personally and spiritually. But just as importantly, prisoners offer gifts to us. Members of our congregation have learned about themselves in surprising ways through interactions with prisoners. In certain moments, those of us involved stumble upon freedom. Building community with prisoners helps free them from the dehumanizing routines of prison culture and helps us on the outside overcome our preconceptions and aversions.

Working with prisoners helps free us from cynicism and despair. If you want to learn how to keep hope alive, involve yourself with the voiceless ones, with the infinitely oppressed. Involve yourself with the desperate, the unloved, the wretched, the thrown-away souls. There you will find hope and compassion; you will find astonishing art and wisdom. Prisoners will remind you that even here, even now, even in the darkness, the spirit is strong, the spirit is free, and the dignity of being human is alive with possibility in every moment. You will be reminded that it is self-indulgent to lose hope in your relatively privileged circumstances. You may even be inspired to create a better world for free men and women to step into once they are released.

Finding Freedom with Prisoners

IN A SOCIETY THAT REGARDS prisoners as wasted lives to be ware-housed away without significant resources for rehabilitation, the work of building community with prisoners has to start with the question, why bother? Is there not an endless list of injustices in the world crying out for social change? There are plenty of oppressed groups that may seem more deserving of our commitments, resources, and support than prisoners. Prison work involves us with men and women who have made serious mistakes, sometimes with terrifying consequences. Why should we intervene to mitigate their punishment? There are at least three compelling reasons to become involved with prisoners: to respond to the command of conscience, to promote enlightened self-interest, and to find freedom.

The Command of Conscience

Our Unitarian Universalist affirmation of the inherent worth and dignity of every person and our obedience to the governing force of love in our relationships with one another command us to reach out to the voiceless. These religious principles underlie the Unitarian Universalist Association's 2005 Statement of Conscience: Criminal Justice and Prison Reform (see p. 75). The UUA Commission on Social Witness guides a four-year process in which social justice concerns are studied and acted upon by member congregations,

1

culminating in an official statement by the association. The 2005 Statement holds that "the magnitude of injustice and inequity in [the U.S. prison] system stands in stark contrast to the values that our nation—and our faith—proclaim."

More than two million human beings who are locked behind walls in America have little power to change the circumstances of their imprisonment. Most will not win their freedom through the judicial appeal process. Most will not find compassion, justice, equality, or encouragement for spiritual growth in the prison society to which they are confined. Their search for truth and meaning will be limited by the controlled and censored environment of the penitentiary. The basic values of our faith are systematically denied to prisoners in a way that no other group experiences. Faith communities are called by conscience to respond.

There are many ways to work for change, of course: writing letters to elected representatives, collecting clothing or belts for prisoners released in ill-fitting clothes, holding protests or vigils against the death penalty, providing services to families and children of prisoners, demonstrating outside state capitols, educating ourselves about prisons and prisoners, and circulating e-mails about prison issues. All these and other forms of advocacy are important ways to make a difference. The Thoreau Congregation's energies are drawn toward direct contact with prisoners. Whatever initiatives we choose to take, people of conscience are called to action.

Over two million people in the United States are incarcerated (not including those arrested under the broad category of "terrorism" since the Patriot Act went into effect). We imprison more people per capita than any other nation in the world, 714 prisoners out of every 100,000 in the general population. The U.S. prison system can be viewed as a form of institutionalized slavery, a race-and-class-based system of injustice designed to lock up poor people with substance abuse problems, mental illnesses (including mental retardation), and histories of abuse and neglect. Most prisoners in the United States would be in treatment programs of various kinds if they'd had the good fortune to be born into middle-class or upper-middle-class homes, or if they'd been born poor in other developed countries.

Our congregation does not advocate tearing down all prisons and releasing everyone in them. Prison guards sometimes joke about naïve volunteers who come to the jails to "hug a thug" and then safely retreat to their homes and churches feeling better about themselves. Ours is not one of those programs. Although we vow to respect the worth and dignity of every person, it is clear that many people in prison pose, or at one time posed, a danger to other people. Some prisoners are violent, full of rage, and unable to control their impulses. We don't claim that every prisoner is wrongfully convicted or would profit from therapeutic treatment.

Penitentiaries, as originally envisioned by members of the Quaker faith, were places where people who had harmed others could reflect on their behavior, become penitent, and change their lives. However, the prison system in the United States does not function in this way. Justice is not always served. The so-called War on Drugs in the United States has criminalized addictive behavior among poor people, while looking the other way at addictive behavior in those who can afford expensive lawyers. Sex workers, some of whom are themselves victims, are criminalized. Abused women are often criminalized for defending themselves or their children from their abusers.

Prisons perpetuate violent practices and create climates of hostility where it is not easy to reflect, to experience penitence, or to turn lives in a positive direction. Ex-prisoners have great difficulty finding housing, jobs, education, or support systems for reorganizing their lives. Churches engaged in prison work cannot solve all the problems of the prison system. Still, as members of a small Unitarian Universalist congregation, commanded by conscience, we set out to do what we could.

Enlightened Self-Interest

Not all members of our congregation are called to prison work based on religious principle. There are other, more pragmatic reasons to work with prisoners. For instance, the overwhelming majority of prisoners will re-enter our communities. Thus, what Alexis de Tocqueville called "self-interest rightly understood" impells us to increase our security and prosperity by contributing to the success of released prisoners. Studies by the Federal Bureau of Prisons, the Texas Department of Criminal Justice, and numerous academic researchers consistently find that prison education dramatically reduces rates of recidivism. Prison education is expensive, but the cost savings associated with lowering recidivism and turning out productive, tax-paying citizens far outweigh the costs.

Emphasizing the practicality of criminal justice and prison reform, the 2005 Statement of Conscience calls for programs based on rehabilitative and restorative justice. Rehabilitative justice is defined as "a process of education, socialization, and empowerment of the person to the status whereby she or he may be able to contribute constructively and appreciably to society." Restorative justice allows offenders to reconcile with victims "through appropriate restitution, community service, and healing measures."

In a political environment where these approaches are all but absent from public policy, the most pragmatic approach may be for concerned people to create such programs themselves. In the subsequent chapters, readers will find the story of how one congregation did just that.

Freedom as a Quality of Being

Some of us who work with prisoners have learned that opening ourselves to relationships with prisoners is a way to find freedom. The phrase "finding freedom" comes from the title of a book by Buddhist practitioner Jarvis Masters, who lives on San Quentin's death row. Masters and many other thinkers have discovered that freedom is possible in a cell, just as people outside of prisons, with all the trappings of freedom, can feel imprisoned in various ways.

From a political and legal standpoint, freedom is an objective condition that most people are able to enjoy. But freedom is also a quality of being in the world. We are, to a greater or lesser extent, slaves to our thoughts, feelings, and preconceptions. Free minds can exist and thrive in prison. Building communities of trust, respect, and shared meaning with free-world people (as non-prisoners are called in prison lingo) can encourage this possibility. Working with prisoners can also help free those of us on the outside from our fears and prejudices. Directly sharing with prisoners, being present to them, and encouraging their spirituality and our own teach profound lessons about the principles that we espouse.

As Bo Lozoff, founder of the Prison-Ashram Project, wrote in *It's a Meaningful Life: It Just Takes Practice,* "If we are unskilled, self-centered, addicted, or greedy, we will not be very free." Freedom is found in relationships. Building community with prisoners helps us all recognize and act out of our deepest selves, whether we conceive of this place as Buddha-nature, Christ-consciousness, or just as acting from our best selves.

Uncommon Community

Building community with prisoners is not a simple task. Prison authorities and prison culture discourage meaningful relationships. Most prisoners are not accustomed to community participation. Those of us engaged in prison work have heard many prisoners' stories. Few of the prisoners we know had safe, intimate relationships with healthy people in their lives before coming to prison. Few had access to public gathering places and community decision-making structures. Few were engaged with institutional structures such as schools, churches, interest groups, and clubs that nurtured them to imagine and achieve their goals. Instead, their relationships to such institutions were more commonly distant, isolating, and alienating.

Even from the privileged position of middle-class life, building community is a challenge in our society. We try to create communities of trust, respect, and shared meaning within our churches and in other primary relationships. It's not so simple there, either. For example, our own congregation, Thoreau, does well at intellectual stimulation, planning, celebration, worship, and music, but despite efforts to build a small-group ministry program, most members are not integrated into intimate, spiritually open groups. Americans live in a culture of isolation, and we carry that into our churches. In a Sunday morning discussion group at Thoreau one member asked whether any among the twenty of us knew how many times he had been married. None did. "On the street where I grew up," he said, "everyone would have known."

In another example of the challenge of building community, the Thoreau Congregation experienced a rash of thefts in the spring of 2004. Someone was stealing cash from purses. No police were called. Instead, Rev. Bill Clark asked from the pulpit for the person who was committing these thefts to come forward. An adult in our community did come forward privately. A process of restitution and reconciliation began. The victims decided what would constitute restitution. The community managed to reach a loving resolution. The person who had broken the community's trust remained anonymous to all but the parties immediately involved. The broken trust began to repair.

It is easy to regard those in prison as somehow fundamentally different from citizens on the outside. It is natural to think of prisoners as lawbreakers, to wonder what crime placed them in prison. It is easy to forget that the free world is also populated by lawbreakers. Probably the majority of people on the outside are lawbreakers of greater or lesser offense. Variously, they gamble, they drink and drive, they steal, they cheat on their income taxes, they commit acts of violence, they violate OSHA regulations, they dump toxic waste, they hire prostitutes, they steal supplies from their offices, they inflate expense accounts, they skirt employment laws, and they dope themselves. Most lawbreakers do not get arrested; far fewer go to prison.

Nor is it always the degree of criminality that separates what middle-class people regard as "us" from what they think of as "them." There are men and women in prison for crimes that are less serious than stealing money from purses in a church. Middle-class society is characterized by rampant lawbreaking. What mainly separates the middle-class "us" from the working-class or under-class "them" is privilege. The privileged are not systematically policed. The privileged are presumed innocent of lawbreaking in their daily lives. The privileged are integrated into communities that have the resources to settle disputes and breaches of trust, to give support to those who are addicted, suffering, or unable to pay their bills. We all live in a system of law and order where the distinction between those assumed to be likely criminals and those assumed to be upstanding citizens is almost wholly artificial and highly racialized.

Prison work helps build social capital. This concept was popularized by Robert Putnam's essay "Bowling Alone: America's Declining Social Capital" in the *Journal of Democracy*. Putnam defines social capital as "the collective value of all 'social networks' and the inclinations that arise from these networks to do things for each other." Political capital creates power. Economic capital produces wealth. Social capital builds networks of reciprocity, people joining together to help one another. Putnam decries the increasing isolation of Americans, measured by declining participation in civic life. Social capital, he argues, is essential for the preservation of a free society.

Voluntary associations check the power of the state by reducing the need for government programs and by bridging social divides to create community cohesiveness. The academic literature on criminal justice emphasizes the benefit of social capital for crime prevention and for re-entry from prison to the free world. As a society we need to build an uncommon community that supports the spiritual, emotional, and material needs of citizens before they get to prison, instead of within prison and after prison.

It is encouraging that the UUA and many congregations have decided to take on prison work as a social action project. No area of focus could be more relevant to social justice work in each county, state, and throughout the nation. Some people need to be locked up. Many, many others are locked up for crimes no worse than those our friends, family members, coworkers, or members of our churches have committed. Every person is better than the worst thing he or she ever did.

The prison work described in this book will not root out injustice from our society, but it can affirm the human dignity of those who suffer injustice. Our prison work can erode the myth that those on the inside are fundamentally different from free-world people. Once that myth is dispelled, life on the outside begins to look different, too.

THE PROGRAMS

Love creates its own freedom from imprisonment, has its own direction, moves according to its own rhythms, and makes its own music.

—from "Personal Prisons" by Charles (Tom) Brown

The Letter Project

From the cold hands of guards
Flocks of white doves
Handed to us through the bars,
Our hands like nests hold them
As we unfold the wings
They crash upward through
Layers of ice around our hearts,
Cracking crisply
As we leave our shells
And fly over the waves of fresh words,
Gliding softly on top of the world
Flapping our wings for the lost horizon.
　　　　　—"Letters Come to Prison"
　　　　　　　by Jimmy Santiago Baca

IN FEBRUARY 2003, Ray Hill spoke to the Henry David Thoreau Unitarian Universalist Congregation about Texas prisons and what Hill calls the prison-industrial complex. Hill is an openly gay activist, performance artist, and former prisoner who for more than twenty-five years has hosted a radio program called *The Prison Show*. Hill says that among prisoners' greatest needs is contact with free-world people. The culture of prison is degrading and violent;

guards are often abusive and insulting; health care is appallingly substandard; prisoners dare not confide in one another.

The longer a prisoner is institutionalized, the more forbidding the free world becomes. Some prisoners have never seen cell phones, never touched computers, and have spent years without opening a door, seeing children at play, walking outdoors barefoot, or using an alarm clock. Their lives are regulated by loudspeakers, clanging metal doors, and lights that turn on and off at prescribed times. One of the reasons prisoners become repeat offenders is that they lose touch with the skills free-world people take for granted. Establishing a letter-writing friendship with someone in the free world takes prisoners beyond the bars and into the lives of people who have everyday freedoms that prisoners need to know about if they are going to survive outside prison and create healthy lives for themselves after their terms are over.

On the other hand, busy free-world people who establish letter-writing friendships with prisoners often discover that what they and their friends seem most to lack—time—is what prisoners have in abundance. Prisoners think long and deeply about the letters they get; they offer life experience that gives fresh perspectives on their free friends' lives and conflicts; they ask challenging questions about faith, belief, dreams, and plans. Through letters prisoners can give free people a chance to bridge the class gap that is so difficult to cross in person. Few middle-class free people have close, equal, friendships with people whose class, education, and work experiences are completely different from their own.

Prisoners come from all backgrounds, but most come from poor or dysfunctional families. They rarely interact with "square people" who live in homes with books, who have dinner-table discussions about politics and ethics, and chauffeur their children to music lessons, team sports, movies, and malls. Most square people lack the skills to survive in prison or on the mean streets of our cities and may lack what prisoners consider to be common sense or street smarts. They may also be trapped in a middle-class ghetto that limits the range of possible solutions they can see to their problems in life.

Ray Hill convinced some of us in the Thoreau community that writing to prisoners could expand our views of the world, our notions of what it is to be free, and our awareness of the ways we imprison ourselves. Writing to prisoners could help us live our lives and help prisoners pass their time.

Kendall, a member of the Thoreau Congregation who had worked in creative-writing and theater programs in prisons in South Africa, Massachusetts, and Louisiana, asked Ray Hill if she could appear on his radio show and propose something called the Letter Project. In her first appearance on *The Prison Show* she explained that this was not a typical pen-pal program centered on developing romantic interests. There are hundreds of such programs that often end up being a source of mutual predation, in which prisoners attempt to seduce women, and lonely free-world people (men and women) assume fake identities in order to seduce prisoners and indulge in fantasy relationships. Therefore, we never used the term *pen pal* in any discussion of our program. Kendall emphasized that our intention was to cultivate mutually respectful friendships between free and imprisoned people. She invited prisoners to write to her at the radio station. In the first week she received over three hundred letters. She went back on the air the following week to ask prisoners to stop sending them, but by then there were a hundred fifty more.

Warned by Hill that some prisoners might take the opportunity to run scams on unsuspecting people, Kendall drew up some safety guidelines, including using aliases and the radio station address. About thirty members of Thoreau had offered to correspond with prisoners. Kendall randomly distributed unopened letters to these volunteers and took the remaining letters to the community college, where she taught English composition. She offered her students extra credit if they wanted to write to the prisoners.

Before giving the letters to her students, Kendall read and screened the remaining letters to identify prisoners with sufficient writing skills to make the letter-writing worth composition credit. She discovered that despite her warnings on the air, many of the prisoners, familiar with numerous pen-pal programs, were angling for romantic attachments or for people to send them spending money. In addition, some prisoners, knowing nothing about Unitarian Universalism, the banner under which the project was announced, claimed to be seeking fundamentalist Christian friendships. Kendall eliminated the inappropriate letters, sent form letters to those who she declined on, and returned to the Thoreau volunteers with possible alternatives to the correspondence they'd originally received. She fine-tuned the guidelines with input from several members of the congregation and a number of her college students. In addition, the church funded the rental of a post-office box nearby, saving the weekly forty-five minute drive into downtown Houston to pick up mail at the radio station. All this preliminary work took about three months before the program began.

As members of the congregation began developing real friendships with their correspondents, certain questions arose. Should we have set a timeline for the commitment to write letters? What about the guilt that sets in when we owe our friends in prison a letter or two and can't seem to find time to write? If a member of the imprisoned community should be released and want to join Thoreau, how should we welcome this person? (This has not yet happened.) We never asked our imprisoned friends to discuss their crimes, but what if some of them are sex offenders? The members of Thoreau who were writing to prisoners organized a discussion group that met regularly for a few months. We discussed the safeguards already available through the UUA (and the unsettling fact that anyone in the congregation could be a sex offender), shared our joys and concerns, and continued the project.

Pitfalls and tips

We encountered several difficulties as the program progressed. After a couple months of exchanging letters, we invited members of the church taking part in the project to meet once a month to discuss some of the challenges. As part of the review process,

Kendall also received written feedback from the prisoners participating in the program. We learned several lessons as a result.

Randomly distributing unopened letters from prisoners to correspondents was a definite mistake. Prisoners, like free-world people, have varying backgrounds, interests, and abilities to communicate in writing. Finding a good match is not easy and should not be left to chance. Someone, or a small group, should take responsibility for reading all incoming correspondence from prisoners, allowing interested free-world correspondents to choose from the ones that seem most inviting.

Not setting time commitments was another mistake. By establishing time boundaries, correspondents can be free to lengthen their relationship if that suits them, but there would be a clear expectation of a minimum period of time of writing. This helps prevent free-world correspondents from feeling overwhelmed by guilt when they find that their imprisoned friends have more time to write and come to expect more than they can provide. One year is a reasonable time commitment to set up front.

Most of the original correspondences naturally tapered off after about a year and a half, though some prospered for much longer and a few continue to this day. While all prisoners who wrote to students in Kendall's class enjoyed the contact, they found the length of a semester too brief to establish a meaningful relationship. Later, Kendall developed a different project involving students and prisoners, the Writing Mentor Program (see p. 55).

Many free-world correspondents came to regret the use of aliases. Using first names would have been equally safe and would not have involved a level of pretense and distance. Free-world correspondents had prisoners' full names, ID numbers, and addresses, while prisoners didn't even know the true first names of those they were supposedly building friendships with. Prisoners understood full well why people embarking on letter-writing relationships with convicted felons should not volunteer their full names, home addresses, and places of work, but the use of fake names introduced a level of distance, and even mistrust, that became more uncomfortable as the relationships deepened.

One question many free-world correspondents grappled with, though curiously it never seemed to arise for prisoners, was, "What can we talk about?" People who want to write to prisoners may find it helpful to meet with one another before beginning the project to brainstorm some questions that would be mutually enriching to explore in letters with prisoners. Barbara Hamilton-Holway's *Evensong, Volume I* poses many useful questions: What specifically gives me joy? What am I afraid of? What do I believe? What did my parents believe? What's my idea of failure or success? What do I like about myself? Who are the people who have made a difference in my life? Has my life been changed by specific historical events, books, songs, or poems? What do I wish I had done differently? What key events in my life have made me who I am? What mistakes have I made, and what have I learned from them? What decisions do I need to make right now, and what factors am I weighing in those decisions? What questions do I have about myself as a parent, a partner, or a friend? What do I miss? What do I still want to accomplish? Or, as Mary Oliver asks at the end of her poem "The Summer Day," "what is it you plan to do / with your one wild and precious life?"

At the same time the Letter Project got underway, the Thoreau Congregation prepared to begin a small-group ministry program among our members. As we explored possible themes for our small groups, we also discovered an intriguing range of topics to explore in our correspondence with prisoners:

- Tracing our spiritual lineage: Who are our teachers and models?
- What are the vows we live by? How do we create new vows?
- What has been my spiritual journey (perhaps broken into five- or ten-year pieces)?
- Leaving the teacher or teaching: spiritual paths I have left, and what I've learned from them.
- Exploring loving kindness. What is loving? What is

kindness? How does each of us live the intention to be filled with loving kindness for ourselves and others?

- Does altruism exist, and if it does, do we want to practice it?
- What is mindfulness, and how does each of us live out our intention to become daily more mindful?
- When have I felt most cared for? How do I care for myself? How do I care for others? Where is the balance?
- Exploring identity: How has my spiritual journey been shaped by identities I was born with (gender, sexual orientation, ethnicity, class, etc.)? How has my spiritual journey been shaped by identities I have chosen? When is identity strengthening and when is it limiting?
- Illness and accidents as teachers: cancer, stroke, heart attack, head injuries, addictions, etc., and what they teach us.

Probing these questions with prisoners can be deeply enriching and can solve the problem of what to do when an initially exciting correspondence begins to play itself out or become repetitious.

Correspondence with prisoners need not be restricted to language. Prisoners often draw and send pictures. A letter project might give free-world people a chance to make collages, computer art, stick drawings, or finger paintings that express their feelings. Prisoners in solitary confinement don't have access to newspapers and enjoy receiving clippings. Picture postcards or pages torn from *National Geographic* or old calendars become welcome cell decorations and may convey ideas or emotions we don't have words for.

Guidelines should be agreed upon before beginning a letter project, but they should not be interpreted as hard and fast rules. It is important that prisoners, most of whom long for commissary luxuries such as deodorant and the occasional candy bar, do not come to expect free-world community members to be easy targets for quick cash. Money can be a barrier to honest friendships between those who have more than enough and those who have little or nothing. However, if the free-world correspondent, having established a firm and mutually beneficial friendship, wants to send the occasional ten or twenty dollars to the prisoner's commissary account, that should not be regarded as a violation of policy.

In Texas, prisoners are allowed to receive paperback books or stationery mailed by approved vendors, such as major book stores or office-supply stores. Such gifts may foster prisoners' education and ability to correspond and should certainly be encouraged, but most states do not allow prisoners to receive gifts other than clippings, pictures, and money. Restricted items often include stamps, care packages, or books mailed by individuals.

We also learned that free-world correspondents need to be wary of sending gifts to prisoners from online sellers. Kendall has ordered books for prisoners online and frequently prisoners receive the books along with invoices that include Kendall's home address and part of her credit card number. The prisoners who receive these gifts and invoices have always been generous and trustworthy enough to treat her information with respect, but they have also warned her about sending books from online sellers to prisoners she doesn't know well.

Prison mail rooms are public spaces. All prisoners' mail is subject to being read by any number of guards or trustee prisoners before it is delivered. Several books ordered from approved vendors were rejected by prison censors for reasons we could not understand. Censorship seems inconsistent and arbitrary: Some censors reject books with racial epithets in them, regardless of context; some reject books that describe conditions in other prisons, real or fictional. When a book is rejected, the prisoner to whom it was sent is required to pay the postage to return the book to the vendor. As far as we know, none of our letters were censored or destroyed intentionally, but it is not unusual for a letter from a member of our congregation to be "lost in the mail," and the same is true for prisoners' letters to us.

Because of the public nature of correspondence with prisoners, our precautions against sending prisoners our full names and home addresses allowed us to feel safe from unwelcome attention from prison guards or prisoners we didn't know and trust. In the early stages of the project, a prisoner reported that some photographs sent to him were stolen or mutilated by people who intercepted the photos in the mail room, so we decided that our guidelines would include not exchanging photographs. However, over the years we have been doing prison work some of us have exchanged photographs with prisoners, and none of them have been stolen or mutilated.

In fact, once trust has been established, photograph exchanges (even sending photos of pets) can sometimes deepen connections or at least to allow us visual images (sometimes quite surprising) of those with whom we have developed spiritual relationships. We remain cautious, however, about sending photographs of our children, and doing so is always a matter for personal discretion. Overall, it is necessary to have guidelines, but individual correspondents, after six months or more of trust-building, can depart from the guidelines as they see fit.

What participants have to say

The following responses are culled from written feedback about the program from congregants and prisoners, and from the letters themselves. These are worth quoting at length because the statements allow us to look directly into the personal relationships that developed during the first year of the letter exchange.

It strengthened me by taking me away from prison issues, if only for a short while, letting me deal with others who have no knowledge of convicts except what the media portrays. It caused me to think, listen, exercise my mind on life outside these walls.
—Johnny Ray (prisoner)

The project has helped me connect to a sense of humility and gratitude for the circumstances of my life. It has given me a view of an incredible person, a gentle spirit, locked away like an animal. It has renewed my outrage at the criminal "justice" system in this country. It has given me more motivation to work for changes in this system.

—Rhoda (free world)

For an inmate to be able to have an opportunity to share his intellect in a positive way is a valuable gift—especially in an oppressed and negative environment like we live in.

—Bill (prisoner)

Letters fall like manna from heaven onto the stainless steel table below my cell, where they're sorted for distribution. Words are my lifeline, my last defense against the ever-advancing crush of isolation. I reach for a clean sheet of paper. I sense freedom in its blankness.

—Rick (prisoner)

I just lost my dad a few weeks ago after a long illness, and Keith, who is serving a long sentence on a drug charge, helped hold me up through his strong spirituality. He's been experiencing a lot of frustration over things happening with his family, which of course he has very little control over, and I think my letters and words of encouragement have helped him through it. We've discussed the idea of conducting a little one-on-one writing workshop through the mail, and we're both looking forward to starting that.

—Clint (free world)

My friend on the outside enjoys our letters. I do too! I love our conversations because they are of value, as opposed to wasted breath in here on topics such as dope, crime, and baseless complaints. The repetitive nature of these topics, as well as the paranoia this environment cultivates, is like a yoke strapped to my neck. It's diffi-

cult to continuously keep a positive outlook and progressive focus, but I try! And she helps me, so I thank her! Her compassion and strength blaze like an inspired thought. Try'n to hold onto that is like hugging a cloud. She's an exceptional person, but she's too hard on herself. I have told her, "Don't judge yourself by others' standards. Look for the joy in your life and that which you create in others. Measure your heart's content and the passion with which you live." She listens to me sometimes.
    —Jesse (prisoner)

I am learning that I have lots and lots of masks that I wear around almost everyone—by writing to Mark I am able to dig deep into the raw emotions and explore them. He is an extraordinarily sensitive and emotional man—he knows just the right "buttons" to push to take me beyond the superficial and into what really matters.
    —Irma (free world)

I feel important. I don't know why somebody who doesn't even know me would take the time to write and get to know me, but it's cool. I've never known anybody like the guy I'm writing to. He's like people I only used to see in the street. I wondered what made them tick. Now I'm actually talking to somebody who wears suits to work. He's not so different from me. He worries about his kids and his old lady. He wonders if he's going to get laid off. He feels lonely sometimes. He likes to get letters from me.
    —John C. (prisoner)

This correspondence is helping me deal with some of my own demons and straightening out some preconceived notions I had regarding "cons." My guy made it clear he wasn't interested in a very short correspondence, as he had been left out in the cold by so many previous pen pals. In doing so, he pulled something out of me, because I had to take pause and ask myself if this was really something I wanted to do. It is, and that makes me feel good. I definitely have been surprised at the depth of feeling this whole thing has inspired, and how much I think my inmate and I have gotten out of the project.

—Steve (free world)

The best part of the program is the interaction with people in the world, other than family and friends. This allowed me to look at their thoughts and to express my thoughts to them. I was surprised, every letter I got.

—Fred (prisoner)

I didn't know that the prison had no air-conditioning and no heat. I didn't realize how hungry the inmates are on a regular basis. I didn't understand how the commissary worked. I just assumed they were issued hygiene products and clothing. It is very dismal. TV shows depict the "luxury" life inmates lead—cable TV, workout facilities, etc. This is not the experience that Joe is having.

—Johanna (free world)

[My free-world correspondent] stated that he would share his spiritual journey toward his present community if I was interested. Well, I'm interested. I want to know all about his community and its belief system. Most people look for differences to either criticize or show superiority. I like to look for similarities in our faiths.

—Jeff (prisoner)

Ramon's childhood and early adulthood are quite similar to mine. My father was a heavy drinker and often beat on my mother and me. As a child, I can remember many nights in my room, afraid to come out because of the yelling my parents were doing. In my adolescence, I rebelled. I dropped out of the eleventh grade and went to work in a series of blue-collar jobs. During the weekends, evenings, and when I wasn't working, my life looked much like what Ramon describes. One of the interesting differences between Ramon's childhood and mine is that my parents did not split until after I was out of the house. In addition, I always believed I could do great things if only I wanted to. This was part of the mix that provided me with the motivation to go to college, to get a bachelor's degree, and to go to graduate school and earn my PhD. In my gut, I believed I could do it if I wanted to. Part of this may have been that I was white and male. Part of it may have been that my mom was willing to pay my college tuition. I was given a few breaks in difficult situations that others, of a different skin color, would most likely not have been given. These are the situations of which I am aware. In many other ways of which I am not aware, I suspect that my social position provided me with forgiveness and opportunities not afforded to others. My correspondence brings all of this up for reflection in new ways.

—Mike (free world)

This sampling of responses to the Letter Project conveys some sense of its importance to the prisoners and free-world correspondents, but there are aspects of the project that defy brief description. Many prisoners, partly in an effort to remain sane and keep their spirits alive and partly as a way to fill the time, develop their skills as artists, philosophers, and counselors, and their generosity is as boundless as their need for human contact outside the world of criminals and guards. Many prisoners send their friends in the free world beautiful pencil or pen-and-ink drawings, painted handkerchiefs, handtooled wooden pens made in prison craft shops, handmade birthday or holiday cards, woven holiday ornaments, and poems.

Their friends on the outside send them newspaper clippings, books, stationery, postcards, or cards for birthdays and holidays. Many prisoners have been abandoned by family and friends, and some say these cards are the only ones they have received in many years. They take pride in decorating their cells with them until the next shakedown, when guards come through and empty their one drawer full of possessions onto their bunks, tear down their wall decorations, and confiscate their personal belongings.

Exchanging letters and gifts is an opportunity for spiritual growth for both correspondents. A prisoner named Guillermo,

who was in solitary confinement for fourteen years, asked his correspondent, "How have your life experiences shaped who you are?"
She answered his question as best she could and then asked him
the same question in return, adding the follow-up question, "And
what do you want to do with the time you have left?" Guillermo
answered with this letter:

> If these people make me do my whole sentence, I'll be forty
> when I get out. Still time left, but that's living in the future,
> and I've done a lot of my time that way. Come to think of it,
> I've lived most of my life that way. When I was fourteen and
> fifteen I would say to myself, "When I grow up I'll do this or
> that." When I first came down [to prison] I would console
> myself when the riots, gassings, and shakedowns started or
> when I got a visit from my kids and they'd ask me, "When
> you coming home, Dad?" I'd say, "When I make parole in
> eighteen months, like my court-appointed lawyer promised
> me." That was fourteen years ago. I was always living for a
> parole date. Last month the parole board turned me down
> again and gave me a four-year setoff [four years before they
> will consider my request for parole again].
>
>   Sitting here thinking of this brings on a dark anger and
> rage. Even knowing I put myself here with what I did, it still
> pisses me off. I'd be lying if I said I didn't feel these dark
> emotions. I don't want to be a bitter person, and I know if I
> hang onto these feelings I will be one. So where do I go from
> here? It's not so bad here in the penitentiary, so I'll just keep
> working on myself as I've been doing all these years. I've even
> come to enjoy this time by myself with my books. As I sit
> here and write you, nothing is missing.
>
>   I wish I could be out there so I could pull on my son's ear
> and tell him that ain't the way. But I'm not there, and nothing
> I can do will change that. That's hard, extremely hard. Like
> I told you in my last letter, it feels as if I'm abandoning my
> kids. Have you ever noticed how we know better, but we still
> run our heads against a wall, e.g., you running yourself till

you neglect your body and loved ones, and me not letting go of these emotions I know bring me harm? Maybe I'm a closet masochist and secretly want to be punished? Like you, I'm curious, and it's a shame I didn't rediscover that till I was put in this cage. I have this wonder for this world, its history, and its people. I love people. I love the drama we create in our lives. I love people with all our flaws and warts. Even the ones I want to put my foot up their ass. You said you wanted to know what is the best, the highest, and the finest way to live. That's easy. A condo on Fifth Ave. in New York with a blond-headed broad! Nah, just kidding. I wish I had the answer to that, but till I find it, I'ma try to sit still in this moment and cry when I'm sad and laugh when I feel joy. Thank you for being my friend.

Each prisoner and free-world person has a unique relationship, and each is as different as the participants. One of our correspondents was David Resendez Ruiz, the man who took the state of Texas to court for mistreatment of prisoners and, as the named head of a class-action suit, actually won. Because of Ruiz and those who supported his suit, the Texas Department of Corrections (later named the Texas Department of Criminal Justice), was under federal oversight for twenty years.

During all those years, and until his death in custody in November 2005 from what his correspondent, Kendall, believes was medical neglect, Ruiz was held in solitary confinement. Like many of our imprisoned correspondents, he lived in an underground three-walled cement cell, six feet by nine feet, with a fourth wall of quarter-inch steel gridwork that had a slot near the bottom through which food was shoved. A toilet and sink were in the cell. When he left his cell for a shower, or for recreation three times a week, he had to first put his arms through the food slot and be handcuffed. On the way to the showers or recreation area he was preceded and followed by armed guards. Recreation meant being put in a slightly larger cell with a chin-up bar and a basketball hoop, and sometimes a slightly flat basketball.

Ruiz was incarcerated for most of his adult life, and while in custody he developed hepatitis C and cancer of the liver. Yet he experienced himself as free, because his spirit was free, because he had educated himself and had become a writ-writer (paralegal), and devoted his adult life to activism on behalf of prisoners' rights. He had a sense of purpose and fulfillment that Kendall, his correspondent, says she seeks but seldom finds. Ruiz was a visual artist and poet, and among his many gifts to Kendall were pictures for her daughter's bedroom, handmade cards and Christmas decorations, a woven keychain, and many stories that feature humor, rebelliousness, and inventiveness.

At sixty-two, Ruiz served as friend and counselor to Kendall, encouraging her to get more rest, to take her time, to focus on social action through persistent effort, and never to give up or to blame herself for scant progress. They corresponded for three years, and she visited him in person several times. Kendall found that his presence was as inspiring as his letters. Ruiz walked like royalty, preceded and followed by guards, ushered into yet another cell for a visit through tempered glass and steel mesh. His smile was genuine and his self-esteem was palpable. He spent much of their time together talking about his concern for the rights of imprisoned immigrants, urging her to take up the struggle for the civil rights of all prisoners, suggesting people she could contact and actions she could take.

While minimizing his own health issues and insisting that he kept himself in shape by doing pushups in his cell and jogging in place, he urged his friend to get more exercise and to spend less time behind her desk. When they parted for the last time, they put their hands together on either side of the steel mesh, and he said, "I've had a good life. Maybe I'll beat this liver cancer, or maybe I won't. You've been a great friend to me these last three years. Whatever comes next, I'm ready for it." He left her with this poem, published posthumously in *The Texas Observer* on December 2, 2005:

Night shadows dance on the wall,
I hear the sound of steel on steel
echo and re-echo
through these cold cells.

Officials pace the catwalks,
counting and recounting,
"Ruiz are you there?"
Yes, I am still here.
You laugh. I hear it
echo and re-echo
through these sad cells.

"Ruiz, what do you see,
alone in that cell at night?"

I see your face without its mask,
I see ships full of Blacks in chains,
I see the slaughter of my
Ancestors—
Mexicans and Indians,
I see you steal their lands,
you sit on the face of the poor
in the free world you lock us out
so we steal, then you lock us in
with the sound of steel on steel
that echoes and re-echoes
through these lonely cells.

I see you try to break us
see you isolate and kill,
then call us killers,
call us violent so we escape
a little while: drink, drug
ourselves, for which you
lock us in again, the
sound of steel on steel

echoes and re-echoes
through these bitter cells.

"Ruiz, you just one Mexkin. You
lost your youth, your hair is gray.
What do you think you gained?"

I'm the *huevon* Mexican, cell-taught,
self-taught, the original writ-writer,
chained up and locked down
for a lifetime. I'm the Mexican
who never gave up, who fought till
every prisoner, guard, and lawyer
in America knows me, I taught myself
to use your tools: I'm Ruiz,
unbroken for all your torture,
all your shackles and steel on steel
that echoes and re-echoes
through these dark cells.

When the Eagle killed the Serpent
a Nation was born; when the people rise
my Nation is born: I am
whole in The People's Nation.
The people will judge you, not me.
You are the one trapped
in the sound of steel on steel
which echoes and re-echoes
through these empty cells.

—"Steel on Steel"

How you might do something similar

The Prison Show, broadcast from Houston, Texas, is available live
on the Web at www.kpft.org every Friday night from 9:00 P.M. to
11:00 P.M. (CST), and from 9:00 P.M. to midnight on the first Friday

of each month. The first hour is a talk show on subjects of interest to prisoners and their friends and families; the next hour (or two) is devoted to call-ins from people wanting to communicate with prisoners. In Texas, prisoners are rarely allowed phone calls, except in emergencies. Listeners can call in starting at 9:45; the number is 713-526-5738. Any group interested in starting a letter project can call in, identify the group and its intention, and give a post-office box or other address for prisoners to write to if they are interested in participating.

Those who want to reach prisoners outside of Texas can try one of three options. The first is to correspond with Unitarian Universalists in prison. The Unitarian Universalist Church of the Larger Fellowship (CLF) serves isolated religious liberals, including more than three hundred prisoners who have joined the CLF to receive UU spiritual support by mail. CLF's letter-writing ministry matches prisoner-members with free-world members of any UU congregation for an exchange of friendly letters, and offers ongoing advice and support to all letter-writers. Participation in the fellowship's letter-writing ministry can offer valuable experience to UUs who are exploring options for congregationally based programs for prisoners. Information about the fellowship's letter-writing ministry, including the guidelines that all CLF letter-writers (incarcerated and free-world) agree to follow, can be found at www.clfuu.org/prisonministry or by writing to CLF Prison Ministry, 25 Beacon Street, Boston, MA 02108.

The second option is to access a nationwide list of self-introductions by prisoners seeking pen pals. Some such lists charge a fee. One that does not is LostVault.com. Many of the prisoners on this list are looking for romantic pen pals, but it is fairly easy to determine that from reading their introductions on the website. Prisoners are not allowed access to the Internet but their requests for pen pals are posted by friends and family members. The site also features a discussion board for sharing experiences related to corresponding with prisoners. This site includes many postings from women seeking pen pals.

The third option is to seek out prisoners in your own region. Most prisons have educational programs. A group or individual interested in building community with prisoners could contact those in charge of education at a particular prison and request names and addresses of prisoners looking for an opportunity to expand their horizons or practice their writing skills. In states where educators are not allowed to give out names and addresses of prisoners, a teacher might be willing to post a notice or discuss the program with students in adult-education or community-college classes at the prison. Getting started might require some persistence: If prison educators are not helpful, a chaplain, prison therapist, prison nurse, or any of a number of functionaries right up to the local warden might help spread the word.

All you need to get started is an address (preferably a post-office box) to which interested prisoners can send letters introducing themselves, and a facilitator to pick up the mail and make those introductions available to those who want to write to them. Volunteers might meet and read introductions together, passing them around until each feels he or she has a good match, or someone might make copies of prisoners' introductions and provide packets for people to take home. Once the matches are made, have one or two people check the mailbox every week and put the prison mail in a centrally located place where volunteers can pick up the letters at their convenience.

Prisoners are demonized on TV, film, and in the media. Mass murderers, sex offenders, and cold-blooded pathological liars make good plots for TV dramas. However, most people in U.S. prisons are there because they could not afford effective defense lawyers. They had the misfortune to be born poor, often to parents who were alcoholics or drug addicts, and they never had a good shot at the so-called American Dream. The War on Drugs has contributed to the United States imprisoning more people per capita than any other nation in the world. In her essay "Masked Racism: Reflections on the Prison Industrial Complex," Angela Davis describes this as a class war. She writes, "Imprisonment has become the response of first resort to far too many of the social problems that burden people who are ensconced in poverty. These problems often are veiled by being grouped together under the category 'crime' and by the automatic attribution of criminal behavior to people of color. Homelessness, unemployment, drug addiction, mental illness, and illiteracy are only a few of the problems that disappear from public view when the human beings contending with them are relegated to cages."

According to the 2006 National Survey on Drug Use and Health, 20.4 million Americans age twelve or older have used an illicit drug. The rates of use among whites were similar to rates for minority groups, meaning the overall number of white users was much higher. Yet federal and many state sentences for crack cocaine, which tends to be used by inner-city nonwhites, are up to one hundred times harsher than sentences for powder cocaine, which is preferred by suburban whites. Specifically, under federal sentencing guidelines, possession of five grams of crack cocaine carries a mandatory minimum sentence of five years imprisonment. It takes five hundred grams of powder cocaine to trigger the same mandatory minimum sentence. According to the Bureau of Justice Statistics, at the end of 2005 the rate of incarceration for black men was 3,145 per 100,000 in the United States, compared to 1,244 per 100,000 among Hispanic men and 471 per 100,000 among white men.

Developing a mutually respectful relationship with a prisoner via correspondence is one way to redress the class war by making peace where we stand, by opening our world to receive gifts of insight and poetry we may not imagine. A genuine correspondence offers one prisoner an opportunity to peer into a home and a life that may be substantially different from anything he or she has ever known, and it offers the free-world writer exactly the same opportunity. Building community with prisoners means being an activist against the disparities that separate us from each other. It is more than walking out into no-man's-land and shaking hands, or dishing out soup to the homeless one or two days a year. Building community means sitting down to talk together, over a period of time, about what matters to each of us; it means laughing and crying together; it means marveling sometimes, drop-jawed and amazed at our differences and even more stunned by our commonalities; it means supporting each other in the lonely effort to know who we are and why we are here.

The Writing Workshop

Where I'm from just might leave you stunned
I'm from the projects
I'm from the slums
I'm from where the weak dies and only the strong survives
I'm from the city of pain where everybody and they
      momma
gangbang, I'm from the hood where everybody's up to no
      good
I'm from a family that was dissected into enemies which led
to my ghetto stricken poverty
I'm from 90th Street and Avalon, the corner of the block
where they pack everything from AKs to Glocks
Where I'm from so many people drink and use drugs
I'm from a place where adults teach kids how to be
the best of thugs
I'm from drive-bys, funerals every weekend, cocaine, indo
      weed, triple zero
bags, a creased blue rag, and my pants sag
I'm from the womb of a mother on welfare married four
      times
I'm from the sperm cell of a deadbeat dad
who himself lived a gang-affiliated life
Where I'm from led to where I'm at, a father

with three kids and a X on my back
I'm also from a molding GOD who fashions me
more and more each day
I'm from a life full of drama with a determined
mission today
I'm from juveniles, rehab homes, boot camps until I
was grown
I'm from prison complexes damn near all over Texas
I'm from GED schools, I'm from the it's-
never-too-late-to-learn rule
I'm from college courses and multiple trades, I'm
from Taleem Service and Jumah Friday, I'm from
the religion of Islam praying five times a day
I'm from the visitation room where I made
amends with my family and made everyone happy
　　　—"Where I'm From" by Doyle "Trey" Burns, III

FACED WITH A $10 BILLION budget shortfall in 2003, the Texas legislature imposed cuts across a broad range of social services and educational programs. One politically easy target was prison education. The Windham School District, which runs basic adult-education programs and vocational training for the Texas Department of Criminal Justice, lost 19 percent of its budget over a two-year period, resulting in more than two hundred job losses for the district. Even before the cuts, the school system's programs had slots for only about 56 percent of prisoners. Many other prison programs took direct hits as the prison system's budget was cut by $230 million, or about 5 percent. Things got so bad that the administration ordered prisoners' caloric intake to be cut from 2,700 calories per day to 2,500 as a cost-saving measure.

Not surprisingly, access to higher education is limited for most Texas prisoners. Those who want to take college classes must come up with their own funds to pay for them. In most prison units, once an associate's degree is earned, opportunities for higher education are exhausted. Only a few units offer full bachelor's degree programs and only one offers any master's degree plans. Since the 1990s, Congress has barred the use of federal loans for higher education in prisons across the nation. Such policies are shortsighted, since there is strong evidence that recidivism drops dramatically with each increment of education a prisoner attains. Educating prisoners is good, cost-effective public policy, but it remains politically unpopular.

More than ever, volunteers who work with prisoners fill a void that the states are unable or unwilling to address. Partly in response to the Texas budget cuts, during the summer of 2003 Kendall asked me to work with her to facilitate a creative-writing workshop inside a prison. A professor of drama and English, Kendall had experience with writing programs in prisons in Louisiana, Massachusetts, and South Africa. As a political science professor and a poet, I had never considered doing this kind of work. I was reluctant. Kendall urged me to read some books of prison writings, including *The Funhouse Mirror* by Robert Ellis Gordon and inmates of the Washington State prison system. Before the end of the summer, I was sold on the idea.

Kendall and I put together a proposal and a syllabus and requested an audience with officials from the Texas Department of Criminal Justice and the Windham School District in Huntsville, Texas. It took many phone calls to set this up, but eventually we were allowed to pitch our proposal, and after several delays the idea was approved. We were instructed to enroll for a half-day volunteer training session, which was conducted at the Carol Vance Unit in Richmond, Texas. The Carol Vance Unit is run by the InnerChange Freedom Initiative, a Christian fundamentalist organization that describes itself as "supporting inmates through their spiritual and moral transformation." Volunteers in that unit are required to sign a statement of faith affirming, among other things, that they "believe in one God, Creator and Lord of the Universe, the co-eternal Trinity: Father, Son, and Holy Spirit." Clearly, this would not be a place anxious to welcome Unitarian Universalists leading a writing workshop!

The state volunteer-training program was aimed mainly toward alerting volunteers about security threats as well as typical cons that prisoners might run against them. The prisoners were portrayed as predators and the volunteers as gullible victims. The PowerPoint presentation at the heart of the training session featured one slide admonishing, "Do not fall in love with the prisoners." At this, we would fail spectacularly. It turned out that we came to love nearly all the men in the workshop.

As newly trained volunteers, we were instructed by prison authorities to find a home for our workshop by contacting Windham School District principals at nearby prison units. That was not difficult, given the many prisons in our area. We reached an agreement with the pleasant and supportive Jester III Unit principal, Ron Gentry, who got the approval of his warden. Jester III is a medium-security medical unit sitting on a large agricultural property southwest of Houston near Sugar Land, Texas.

The unit is only a few twists and turns west along Oyster Creek from Sugar Land Central Unit, where Huddie Ledbetter, better know as Lead Belly, is said to have written the famous song "Midnight Special." About half the prisoners at Jester III are assigned there for medical reasons. Many have hepatitis C or HIV. Many more suffer from chronic pain, are amputees, or are wheelchair bound. Many of those assigned to Jester III for nonmedical reasons are placed in the unit for protection from gang violence or other threats. A higher proportion of sex offenders seems to reside there than in other Texas prison units.

We decided that our Writing Workshop at Jester III would meet for three hours each Monday evening and that we would follow the semester schedule of Alvin Community College, which offers classes in this prison and at other units in the region. A Notice to Offenders was posted on bulletin boards in the prison by Ron Gentry, the unit principal, requesting writing samples from interested prisoners. The applicants were vetted for eligibility by the prison based on their behavior, and the remaining applicants' writing samples were turned over to us to decide who would join the workshop. All the writing samples treated fairly safe themes. Some applicants submitted saccharine, rhymed love poems in irregular meter; several others sent in religious essays. Errors in grammar and spelling were common. Out of about twenty applications, we selected eight men as our first students. We believed that all of them showed something that we could work with.

The workshop began in the spring semester of 2004 and continues to this day; at the time of this writing, it has been sustained through eight semesters. Members from previous semesters are readmitted automatically, and when vacancies arise new applications are accepted. One prisoner, a fifty-two-year-old long-timer named Allen Woody, has been with the group all eight semesters. Jerry Loggins, an original member, began the sixth semester, but was suddenly transferred to another prison. Not all applicants have been admitted to the workshop. At times, the waiting list has numbered around ten. About forty men overall have participated during the eight semesters. We raised the capacity of the group from eight to ten, and during part of one semester we allowed the workshop to grow to eleven.

The writing skills and educational levels of the writers vary widely. Some of the men have not finished high school. One, John E. Christ, holds a PhD and an MD. Another, James Baker, is a couple of classes shy of a master's degree. Several have taken all of the associate's level classes available to them in the prison, making our workshop the only higher educational offering they could still take, though it is not for college credit. Their ages range from twenty-two to sixty; they are white, black, Asian, and Latino; they have sentences ranging from two years to ninety-nine; and politically they are conservative, liberal, radical, and apolitical. They are Christians, Muslims, Buddhists, atheists, and Unitarian Universalists; they are former soldiers, doctors, state senatorial candidates, reporters, drug dealers, professional musicians, photographers, and construction workers, among other livelihoods.

Surprisingly, this radical diversity does not produce much conflict. On the contrary, the participants generally maintain an attitude of curiosity and embrace the chance to learn from each other.

The workshop format is simple. Each week begins with a meditation, followed by a check-in, a practice we brought from the Thoreau Congregation. We always address two questions: How was your week? and What did you write? Check-in sometimes lasts a full hour. If we anticipate a busy evening, we ask for a quick check-in. Each week, a piece of published prison writing is distributed and discussed. With rare exceptions, we chose to use only published writing by prisoners as models for the workshop in order to show prisoners that people like themselves can succeed as writers.

After distributing the new reading, we give them a writing assignment that is usually related to the handout. Finally, and most importantly, participants read aloud their writings from the prior week and critique each other's work. As facilitators, Kendall and I complete the writing assignments along with the prisoners. We try to be participants more than teachers. We avoid formal lessons about grammar, punctuation, poetic form, and literary interpretation, although we do not hesitate to allow our knowledge of these things to inform our criticism and advice.

The point of the assignments is not to make a grade or even to meet particular learning objectives. Likewise, the purpose of the class is not to learn specific forms of writing. Indeed, the form is usually left wide open. For nearly every assignment, some men write poetry and some write prose. They sometimes produce drama, raps, and song lyrics. The main instruction is to read the week's handout, to respond to it or write something similar if that seems appealing, or to write something completely different if so inspired. Above all, we stress the importance of paying attention to detail, to words, and to the emotional truth that emerges from the process of writing. Participants simply promise to "show up at the page" and record as truthfully as possible what they encounter.

Something went remarkably right with the initial group of men. Together, we created a free atmosphere for the workshop. We developed close relationships. We removed our masks. This atmosphere has at times been threatened, but we believe it has mainly been preserved throughout the eight semesters, even with rotating membership. To illustrate our remarkable start, the first writing assignment was to produce something about the first day in prison. Julio Castro, a young man from a rural area outside Austin, shared his first draft of this poem at the second workshop gathering:

Entering the first
Rusty barred gate
Instantly intense
Overwhelmed by emotions
Like static
Through the forest at midnight
What to expect
A different country
No communication
Different customs
—"First Day"

Julio was an unsophisticated drug dealer when he entered the "rusty barred gate" of a Texas penitentiary for the first time, not much more than a year before the workshop began. He is a quiet man, shy in a group, not very articulate in his speech, and, although native-born, lacks much understanding of written English usage and grammar. Still, he is infused with an air of eagerness and intellectual curiosity. His astoundingly large, soft eyes are open to anyone wanting a glimpse of his inner nature.

For my part, I also brought a short poem, with the same title, in response to the initial writing assignment. The character named Lucky refers to Julio in this poem:

What mattered was Lucky
trusted us enough to cry.
The circle of writers
propped him up. I hardly recall
bars, clunking locks, or guards.

Julio cried openly on the first night of the workshop. He trusted. He trusted the professors, the killers, the Muslims, the Buddhists, the thieves, the blacks, the whites, the Hispanics. He trusted us enough to cry. Trust in prison is rare. Prisons do little or nothing to create healthy community or to institutionalize trust. The Writing Workshop gives prisoners space to take off the masks they wear to survive inside and, for three hours a week, to explore and reveal their more authentic selves. For reasons that we cannot pinpoint exactly, this openness in the workshop began almost immediately. Perhaps the fact that Kendall and I each shared deeply personal material with the prisoners in our own writings helped to create this space for openness.

In evaluating the Writing Workshop at the end of the first semester, we asked, "What have you gained from this experience that has nothing to do with writing?" Allen Woody, who has been in prison for more than thirty years, answered, "Trust—something that has always been hard to come by in this environment. The fact that everyone involved so freely shared their own experience allowed me to develop at least a part of something I lost many years ago."

Another member of the workshop answered, "Freedom to express myself, my thoughts, a taste of free-world freedom."

We also asked, "What did you learn about yourself?" One man responded, "That I am not anywhere near as isolated in my experiences in here . . . as I had believed. I learned also that there is a long-term benefit from sharing experiences in here with others."

Our initial group included Kenneth Scott, a brilliant young African-American man from the ganglands of Galveston. Kenneth was about thirty years old at the time and near the end of his twelve-year confinement. He was a leader of the Muslim group in the prison and commanded much respect among his peers. In response to the question, "What did you learn about yourself?" Kenneth wrote, "I learned that I am not a true misanthrope. I also learned that I am not as self-made as I thought I was." Here is a poem that Kenneth wrote:

No moan will ever slip my
lips. No tear will ever clear my eyes.
No matter how the anguish
rips, no one will ever see me cry.

I suck up all the pain
and grief; I suck up all the madness.
No one will ever see me
weak. The world only knows my badness.

Hardened by a rain of blows, blackened
by the heat of hate, blinded
by lust of false heroes; all this
I now use to take.

To anybody who would dare to
love me in spite of my crimes:
Don't be fooled to think I don't care.
Inside I'm crying all the time.
                    —"Ballad of a Tough Guy"

Revelations such as these, read in the company of prisoners
from diverse backgrounds, are virtually unheard of in prison and
are incredibly valuable. Many times since the first night when Julio
trusted us enough to cry, tears have been shed openly in the workshop—not only by the men reading their work or sharing their
stories, but also by those of us listening with open hearts. This
level of sharing and emotional support cannot emerge in prison
without a conscious effort to create a space where they are possible.
Few such spaces exist on the inside. In fact, such sharing is rare on
the outside, as well.

During the first semester, Kendall and I met on Monday nights
after the workshop at a coffee shop to talk. Invariably, we were
spilling over with emotion. We noted again and again how this
was so unlike our community-college classes. We marveled at how
much more open and how much freer, more serious, and more
powerful was the prisoners' work. Building trust and eliciting

meaningful reflection in college classes seemed far more difficult than with the prison group. Indeed, neither of us had even thought about building relationships as a key part of our college teaching. The absence of grades in the prison workshop probably contributed to the differences.

In the workshop, it is hard to predict which writing topics will elicit the most meaningful responses. Some successful topics included: where I'm from; my perfect day; portrait of someone I love; why I write; the greatest compassion I ever witnessed; advice for the drive-up (aka the first-time prisoner); scars; and I didn't know I loved [fill in the blank]. This poem by Derek Parks was written in response to the last topic:

> I wish I loved my kids like I love them streets.
> If I spent 100 dollars on shoes, I spent one fifty on weed.
> Can't make it to open house 'cause I'm at the dope house/
> hoe house playing Playstation,
> while the real mothers and fathers are making sure
> their sons and daughters get a viable education.
> I've held guns more times than I've held my kids.
> Got more convictions on my resume than I got gigs.
> Yet I reassure them that I love 'em every time I write—
> a contradiction of my actions? Sure I love them, yeah right.
> Who am I fooling, them or me—Derek be real with yourself.
> You love the money, the drug, the women just like Satan
> himself.
> I love to feel the recoil of a gun's disperse.
> I love the money the game brings every month on the first.
> I love smoking weed quarter pounds at a time.
> I say I'll do anything for my kids but I feel I'm just lying.
> 'Cause see I told 'em I was finished on my last go-around
> be here to raise my sons up, put the guns and dope down
> My life is based on being laced on the latest deceit.
> Man, I wish I loved my kids like I love them streets.
> —"Like I Love the Streets"

Midnight Special

During the summer of 2006, Kendall brought a new idea to the workshop—a proposal that only a dreamer like her would consider: "Let's publish a journal of writings by Texas prisoners edited by Texas prisoners." The participants pounced on the plan with zeal, and the brainstorming began that would give birth to *Midnight Special*. The men in our workshop serve as literary editors, and a crew of volunteers from the Thoreau Congregation help produce and distribute the journal. At the time of this writing, three editions have been published and the subscriber list has grown to more than six hundred.

The publication is named for the Huddie "Lead Belly" Ledbetter song about a train through Sugar Land called the Midnight Special. Legend said that when the light from that train shone on a man in prison, he would soon be free. The journal aims to celebrate the freeing of minds and spirits through words. It validates the talent of the contributors and gives them a venue to share their voices. For the editors from our workshop, working on the journal teaches about the process of submissions and editorial discretion, and creates work that benefits hundreds of readers. For free-world readers, the journal opens a window into the lives of men and women who are effectively silenced and hidden away.

The publication is free for Texas prisoners; free-world subscribers and prisoners from other states are asked to donate ten dollars for the twice-a-year journal. The first two editions were photocopied in an eight-page newsletter format on yellow paper selected to evoke the hue of a train's headlight. Submissions are accepted from any Texas prisoner. Due to space limitations we call for short pieces of writing, limiting submissions to 750 words. Submissions are blind, both to prevent bias and so that they can be distributed to inmate literary editors without violating the Texas rule against inmate-to-inmate correspondence. The works appear under the authors' names, although one author asked that only his inmate number be used, and others have preferred pen names. Payment to the authors is modest: three extra copies of the journal.

Kendall and I code the blind submissions with a number and distribute them to the men in our workshop for editorial review. Sometimes a single submission passes through the hands of several editors for second and third opinions about a piece. The editors are free to accept a work, reject it, or ask that it be revised and resubmitted. They write unsigned letters to the authors informing them of the decision and, when appropriate, offer a detailed critique of the submission. As participants in our Writing Workshop, the men are accomplished in offering constructive criticism.

Midnight Special has created an additional avenue for church members to get involved with prison work. Volunteers type up each issue, check the post-office box, process subscriptions, and print mailing labels. As many as a dozen volunteers have contributed by helping to collate, fold, label, and stamp the journal. We hope to find church members to take on other operations, such as marketing and writing grant applications, that focus on expanding the journal and improving its production quality.

Producing *Midnight Special* has also connected our congregation's outreach efforts to a broader segment of the Texas prisoner population. In January 2008 we published for the first time literary works by a woman prisoner and subscriptions from women began to trickle in. Previously, our connection with Texas prisoners had been limited mainly to those located within listening range of *The Prison Show* on KPFT radio, because this was the way we announced the Letter Project to prisoners. This excluded women, who are warehoused far from Houston. What is clear from subscription data is that as prisoners have been transferred from unit to unit, word about *Midnight Special* has spread all across the state. We've even logged a few out-of-state subscriptions. The letters that arrive requesting subscriptions reinforce the value of the work we are doing. We've heard from, and published, winners of the literary contest for prison writing sponsored by the PEN American Center. We've gotten encouraging thank-you notes praising the quality of the journal and expressing hope for its continuation. More than once, a reader has asked for more information about Unitarian Universalism. Giving voice to the voiceless is powerful and gratifying work. More than anything, this will continue to be our goal.

Pitfalls and tips

The Writing Workshop has not always operated just as we hoped or expected. We've learned some lessons along the way that might be useful to those contemplating similar work. Initially, we hoped that other church members would emulate the workshop idea with proposals of their own to launch workshops in other prisons, perhaps involving creative writing or some other focus. This has not happened. Therefore, our single workshop has been able to reach only a small number of prisoners and has involved only a small number of congregants. At one point, Kendall and I considered splitting our workshop into two groups to maximize its impact, but decided we loved doing the workshop together too much to follow through with this idea.

Recruiting volunteer typists turned out to be a successful means of bringing more church members into the project. About a dozen church members have enthusiastically volunteered for this work, reporting that they enjoy the insights they gain from the authors. This also has served the workshop well by allowing every piece of writing that the prisoners produce in the class to be presented in typed form and copied for distribution to other workshop participants for group criticism. Prior to having the corps of typists, Kendall and I were overburdened with typing, and we did not attempt to type every piece.

There have been some inconveniences. On a few occasions, classes were cancelled because of lockdowns, and other times the prisoners were as much as an hour late due to an earlier lockdown that disrupted the dinner schedule. Sessions are regularly interrupted for "count," when a guard enters the classroom and each of the men calls out his assigned dorm and cell number. Individual prisoners do not always receive the "lay-ins"—printed permission slips—they need to come to the education wing at the appointed time. Once my CD player was prohibited and my CD of prison songs was temporarily confiscated.

Another problem arose when a prisoner, Jerry Loggins, was disciplined for attempting to mail a poem to his daughter that he had written for a workshop assignment. The assignment was to write about the pill line, a perennial focus of complaint in prisons. Jester III, being a medical unit, has an especially long and slow pill line. Jerry's workshop demeanor is serious and respectful, but he writes like the class clown, eliciting plenty of laughs when he reads many of his creations. This is the poem he tried to mail to his daughter:

The Pill Line is a son-of-a-bitch,
causes much more pain than relief.
Men standing—twitching—involuntarily itching
in torment for time beyond belief.

I'd rather hurt, suffer, or die
than stand ten minutes for muted relief.
The pill's a poor portent to being healthy,
listening, looking, learning others' frailties.

Sad eyes, pain-filled, racked countenances,
limping, grunting, shuffling gaits,
stories of mistreatments, unanswered pleas.
No true help, no care, no time to convalesce.

Pills to counter pills to counter pills,
no pills to treat what really ails.
No hope, no love, no soft-spoken words,
just hate, berate, too late to help.

Pill line sucks, all lines suck.
Prison sucks, hurting sucks, dying sucks.
Doctors suck, nurses . . . that'd be okay,
but still all and all it's a son-of-a-bitch.
                                —"A Walk in the Pill Line"

Jerry was disciplined for violating section 42 of the prisoner conduct handbook, which subjects prisoners to disciplinary action for using "indecent or vulgar language or indecent or vulgar gestures in the presence of or directed at an employee or any person." Jerry pleaded not guilty and requested a hearing. At his hearing he pointed out that he had not named any employees, or even the prison, and had not shared the poem with anyone outside the workshop, much less a prison employee. Nevertheless, he was found guilty of the violation and was issued a reprimand, the lightest of possible penalties. Still, the case will remain in the file that will eventually be examined by a parole board.

Kendall and I, along with the prisoners in the workshop, had to decide whether to champion Jerry's cause. One the one hand, this felt like an outrageous violation of creative freedom and a threat to the integrity of the workshop. On the other hand, after a conversation with the school principal, who is responsible for overseeing the workshop, it became clear that he knew nothing about the incident. Challenging the case could have brought negative attention to the workshop and endangered its continuation. We decided that the disciplinary action was most likely a reaction to another recent conflict between Jerry and the prison authorities and the best action in this instance was to do nothing. The next year, Jerry was transferred away unexpectedly.

This incident is an example of the larger problem of creating spaces for creativity within a highly controlled environment. Surprisingly, we have experienced very little supervision inside Jester III. We have never detected any surveillance of the workshop. Except during count, which usually occurs about an hour into our workshop, a guard is never present in the classroom. We were instructed by the Windham School District principal to avoid handouts that described escape, sex, graphic violence, or gang activity. Of course, these topics are not easy to avoid when selecting published writing by prisoners. Nor is it entirely possible, or desirable, to impose limitations on what prisoners can write and discuss. In practice, nobody has ever reviewed our handouts or objected after the fact to literature that we have distributed in the workshop. Kendall and I routinely loan and give away books and magazines to the men. The rather laissez-faire environment that we have enjoyed certainly would not be found in every prison unit.

Grady Hillman, a leader in the international arts and corrections movement with prison workshop experience in many states and several countries, founded the first creative-writing workshop in a Texas prison in 1983. As far as we know, Hillman's ten-month workshop was the only such undertaking in Texas until ours began in 2004. On the topic of surveillance and censorship, Hillman writes in an email,

> In my time working in the Texas Department of Corrections, I very rarely encountered any form of censorship, and guards rarely hung around my workshops. I was initially astonished at the absence of supervision—actually pretty nervous before I got to know the men and had a feel for how the prisons operated. Later, my greatest discomfort was working unsupervised at the women's units and finding myself alone with one of my students.

Hillman goes on to explain that there was a list of censored magazines that weren't allowed into the prisons where he worked, including certain men's magazines and some martial arts guides. Interestingly, *Mother Earth News* was also banned, because it occasionally contains recipes for home-brewed alcoholic beverages. Hillman's workshops were supported by the Committee of Small Magazine Editors and Publishers Prison Project, which sent him boxes of remaindered or donated literary magazines to give to prisoners. As his email continued, Hillman notes,

> I think things are pretty much the same now though there are fewer creative writing programs in adult facilities than there used to be, with the possible exception of county facilities. I think that owes more to the burgeoning privatization of corrections and the elimination of Pell grants for inmates.

Community colleges were a huge presence in the Texas Department of Corrections when I was there. After I quit the residency, I still taught a World Lit course at Ellis [a prison unit] for Lee College. With the exception of Richard Shelton's programs in the Arizona system and what if anything remains in California, most of the state writing programs operate at women's facilities. If I think about it, I can come up with some other men's workshops but they are few and far between. Prison systems no longer make any pretense of rehabilitation so far as I can tell, so there's little pressure to host programs like ours.

And so while prison workshops can enjoy a relative lack of censorship or supervision, they are becoming less prevalent overall. Depending on the nature of the group and the culture of the prison unit, it might be unsafe to broach some topics in some workshops. Much more surveillance would probably be present in some other units in Texas and in some other state prison systems. This obviously would impede the development of open expression and trust.

In some places, the state hires artists to work in prisons. Not in Texas. Kendall and I have discussed our ideological misgivings about volunteering to do what we think should really be the state's work. Ideally, artists would serve on all prison staffs. Realistically, the political capital to make this happen does not exist in Texas or most other places. Until there is a legislative remedy, workshops such as this are not going to occur without volunteers.

The workshop has not always been a love fest of good feelings. There were times when plainly racist sentiments were expressed. There were a couple of short-term participants who were quite unpleasant to be around. Sometimes walls of protectiveness came up around the circle. Racial distrust is profoundly ingrained in prison culture in the United States. Issues related to race are volatile and dangerous because race is so closely tied to gangs in prison. These issues are certainly present in the workshop. There has been no conscious attempt to avoid them, nor are they probed. Once, an African-American participant read a poem with strong anti-Semitic sentiments. A Jewish member of the workshop said he took no offense, but asked if it would be okay to write a poem highlighting stereotypes about African Americans. We discouraged this and fortunately he brought no such poem to the group.

The Jester III workshop is young compared to similar workshops, such as the one run by Hettie Jones at Bedford Hills in New York or the one led by Judith Tannenbaum at San Quentin, among others. Given more time, it might be possible to develop a climate to address racial issues more directly at Jester III. Initially, these issues should be treated with caution.

What participants have to say

The value of the workshop to the prisoners who participated in it is perhaps best expressed by the prisoners themselves. The following quotations are taken from evaluation forms that Kendall and I designed and distributed.

It allowed a great deal of free expression, not only in the class but on assignments. We weren't strictly confined to the topic provided; if we were inspired to write something else, we had the freedom to do so. There was a good spirit of cooperation and camaraderie among the participants that is often lacking in this environment. That spirit will always be of use. Even the hardest exterior often harbors a good heart. [The workshop] brought me out of some of the disappointment I often feel, which is a by-product of doing time. The fact that someone in the free world is willing to devote their time to come in here on a weekly basis, for me, is about as good as it gets.
    —Allen Woody

[The workshop] is an outlet for me to express my feelings and emotions on a variety of subjects. It challenged my creativity. It has allowed me to escape the drab and dreary daily prison routine. It has also brought me into contact with thought-provoking, spiritual, intellectual individuals. I have learned the art of self-expression.

—Perwani

I have been in TDCJ [the prison system] for almost twelve years. The workshop gives me a voice for every facet of my person. I get political freedom (somewhat), comic relief, emotional venting. I have gained faith in myself, self-confidence. My voice has become recognizable and independent. The workshop produced a wonderful Irish stew of personalities. I love every man in our workshop like the brothers we have become. I've seen the politics, streets, homes, fears, and joys of so many from so many diverse backgrounds. I learned that I have something to say that others can enjoy and that I can accept criticism without breaking people's bones. It has given me an outlet for the morass of bullshit I deal with every moment of life on the inside. When I hold things inside I become a simmering pot waiting to boil over. To keep that from happening, and because of this workshop, I can write myself out of the pot.

—Jerry Loggins

The workshop provides a place of mental refuge from the cesspool atmosphere of prison. It has acted as an oasis of freedom inside a box predicated on violence. [The assignments] allowed me to release frustrations and hold forth on topics I normally would not have revealed to anyone in my peer group. I learned that I tend to monopolize discussions. I am predisposed to believing I am right. I gained insight, past the facade of the prison face, into the other members of the group. This allowed me to broaden and temper my opinions of some of my fellow prisoners.

—James Baker

This workshop provided an opportunity to explore ideas and experiences in a meaningful way. I gained a sense of camaraderie with individuals who share like and dissimilar experiences in prison. I have learned I am not really alone in an intellectual prison. I have witnessed deep emotions expressed in the reading of some stories. Expression of one's inner self is not directly related to what is tattooed on the skin. I have been encouraged to continue writing more fervently. I will become a political activist for reform when I am free!

—John E. Christ

I enjoyed the freedom of creativity and the feedback on each other's writing, even the critical stuff. I learned that my writing doesn't suck! [I gained the ability to] accept other people as they are and give people a chance before labeling them. I was really impressed with Aguirre! I didn't know he was so creative. I always thought of him as some hard-nosed Mexican who went balls to the wall. In actuality, he has kept me from getting myself into a mess over stupid stuff. In prison you lose a sense of self and individuality. This class spotlights each individual's thoughts and ideas. Being able to be so different and still work together . . . kind of reminds me of a jazz group. Everybody does their own thing together, and it sounds great.

—Eugene Fitch

I learned how to use writing as a form of therapy. Gaining opinions about your ideas and yourself from others who are outside of your original circle is good so that your evaluation of self will not be biased. Those of us in this workshop have issues that most of the prison population shares, but because of our writing it seems we are dealing with those issues better than the rest of the prison population. More of my inner self comes out in my writing than in my daily speech.

—Abiola

It has made me less afraid to trust others and be more open and free to share. Maybe sometimes we bullshit too much about a lot of stuff. But this is both a strength and a weakness. Being where we are, we are able to let out opinions and thoughts freely without really feeling any apprehensions, as we more than likely would in the dorms. Dr. Kendall and Dr. Speer let me see there are people who are sincere and for real.

—David Aguirre

The workshop challenged me to look into my past in a critical manner and I was able to see how a lot of what I do today is still tied to my past. My self-esteem and sense of self have both increased a lot based on the reception I was given in the workshop and from participating in the dialogues my listening skill and ability to be objective both improved as well. The way I learned to listen and consider other people's points of view is a skill I think I'll be able to benefit from a year from now or even ten years from now.

—Kenneth Scott

How you might do something similar

Starting a prison workshop is an effective way to enter into close relationships with prisoners. Not every congregation will have members interested in literary work, but the workshop model described here can be adapted for other subject matter as well. Many activities can create opportunities for prisoners to share openly, learn humane skills, and create trust. Depending on the resources available for instruction at the prison, workshop topics may include: meditation, yoga, visual art, dance, theater, journalism, book circles, or courses focusing on nonviolence, life skills, financial literacy, or other subjects. Some states may already have workshops that volunteers can join. Otherwise, volunteers may have to propose something new.

For those wishing to research other workshop possibilities, there are a number of helpful publications and websites to consult. The Resources section of this book (p. 83) contains a list of print and Internet resources that we have found to be helpful in our prison work, particularly related to the Writing Workshop. See especially the Community Arts Network website, the PEN

American Center Prison Writing Program on its website and in its publications, and the online article about the Quaker Alternatives to Violence Project.

The Writing Mentor Program

Getting out of myself and serving others is a powerful tool
that, in my experience, was the main key to my transformation in prison. I believe that the world might change for the
better if enough of us shifted our focus toward helping others
who need us. I truly hope that more and more prisoners will
find opportunities for service in their world.

—from *Dharma in Hell* by Fleet Maull

THIS PROGRAM IS ABOUT a radical reversal of the word *mentor* and
the horse it rides in on. Most prison ministry programs assume that
prisoners are deficient in social and moral skills and need mentors
from the free world to sacrifice time and effort to bring them up
to snuff. Our approach puts prisoners in the role of mentors to
college students. Whether self-educated, educated in prison, or
educated in the free world, most of the prisoners we have encountered have more critical thinking skills than the average first-year
college student, and after participating in the mentoring program,
the prisoners were by far the more skilled writers.

The mentoring program was conceived by Kendall, who teaches
composition in college, for use by herself and other composition teachers. With some tweaking and shifting of emphasis, the
program can be adapted for use by parents, counselors, or anyone

involved in human growth and spiritual or intellectual development. It has been used on a small scale by another college professor,
who assigned four PhD students in public policy to imprisoned
mentors to advise them on their dissertation projects in criminal
justice. I employed the approach on a small scale, too, by assigning
prison mentors to comment on papers written by six of my political
science students about conditions in Texas prisons. This chapter
focuses on Kendall's experience during the 2004–2005 academic
year with this program, which evolved from the Letter Project.

As part of the Letter Project, Kendall gave her composition
students the option of earning extra credit by corresponding with
prisoners. Letters from inmates came to a post-office box paid for
by the Thoreau Congregation. Prisoners and students used first
names only, and Kendall read all incoming and outgoing correspondence. Students and prisoners enjoyed the Letter Project, but
they found themselves becoming interested in each other's lives
just as the semester and their period of communication ended.
It was surprising how open they were with each other, given this
limitation. Kendall suggested that in their letters of introduction,
students tell the prisoners who their mentors and role models
were. One student wrote about his grandfather, who encouraged
him to go to college, and the prisoner who received his letter wrote
back,

> Those of us in Seg [solitary confinement] have no access
> to educational programs, so the only way for us to educate
> ourselves is through correspondence, and the colleges don't
> offer written correspondence courses anymore because
> they've all rolled over to computers, which those of us in here
> don't have. I was very impressed with your sharing about how
> your Grandfather's words were very influential on you and
> actually helped you gain in life. I always wanted and longed
> for someone to encourage me. Sad to say, I was raised up by
> a single mom who had problems with alcohol, so I pretty
> much did as I pleased and learned what I could from people

my own age, the blind leading the blind you might say, so I really wouldn't have a success story to share with you, in the form that you shared with me. I wish I did. I never knew any of my grandfathers, may they rest in peace. But I thank you dearly for taking the time to write to me.

The student who received this letter found it difficult to imagine life without computers, let alone a life without a grandfather, but the student and mentor came to understand one another more fully as their correspondence progressed.

Another student was surprised to learn that prisoners in solitary have no access to TV or movies. Her imprisoned correspondent wrote, "We don't have any TV so it's been years since I've seen a movie or TV show, the last movie I seen was a movie called *Young Guns*, it's a cowboy movie. I went to see it in a drive-in theater right before I got arrested." The student had never heard of *Young Guns* and wrote back, "What's a drive-in theater?"

Several of the exchanges convinced Kendall that the extra-credit letter writing was valuable, but she wanted to find a way to make better use of the prisoners' time and talent for her courses. She decided to train a pool of prisoners to comment extensively on students' compositions. It was a way to provide prisoners with some diversion and a chance to contribute to life beyond the prison walls. She also thought it might wake students up and give their compositions more authenticity and real-world purpose.

Kendall solicited free copies of the textbook she uses with her students, sent them to the prisoners in the pool of potential mentors from the Letter Project, and asked the prisoners to write essays. She responded to each of them with the kinds of comments she hoped they would make later in response to students' essays. The comments emphasized what worked in each piece, asking questions that might evoke more detail, and that would relate to the content more than the form. After her responses to their essays, the prisoners revised them and then wrote two-page introductions of themselves to be delivered to their future students. Over the course of this training period, a few potential mentors dropped out, but the ones who stayed became eager to meet their students and get to work.

Eventually, Kendall had twenty-six mentors to work with fifty-two students in two composition classes. Each student had two mentors; each mentor had four students. The mentors commented on three of the six essays students had to write. The schedule was arranged so that there would be time for the essays to get to the prisons, for the prisoners to write responses and mail them back, and for students to hand in revised essays. The program required careful planning, but once it was set in motion, it worked well. Prisoners and students gave the program excellent evaluations.

Pitfalls and tips

The work involved for the teacher was so exhaustive that only an obsessive workaholic could have pulled it off. Kendall was never able to convince another teacher to take on the program in the way she was conducting it. First there was the time invested in training the mentors. Other tasks included monitoring who was mentoring which students, figuring out which essays went into which envelopes, determining how to arrange the whole semester's work around the mailing and receiving of essays, and deciding what to do with late work.

Many of the twenty-six mentors established a somewhat needy relationship with Kendall and wrote her letters that arrived daily. Many included questions she felt she had to answer promptly. Despite stiff penalties, students persisted in turning in late papers. That meant additional mailings to mentors. Some days Kendall sat at her desk in tears, buried in envelopes and handwritten pages. She needed clerical help: a student worker, someone earning service-learning credits, or a volunteer. She needed someone to prepare mailing envelopes, put the essays in the envelopes for each mentor, receive the mentor's responses, sort out which responses went to which class, and keep track of the first and final drafts of each essay.

The project can be simplified. Similar projects can involve as few as ten mentors with roughly five students each; students don't need more than one mentor; and students who turn in late papers should forfeit the opportunity to have a mentor respond to their papers. Given the need for adequate turnaround time through the mail, the mentors can respond to only one or two essays rather than three. The concept is too valuable to be jeopardized by burnout. People developing similar programs can find other ways to simplify the work or can solicit clerical help.

What the mentors and students had to say

In an evaluation at the end of the semester, one student wrote, "Writing to a prisoner helps me with my essays because I can explain them as if I were talking instead of having to write the same old stuff as in high school, where the teacher didn't care how you wrote it or how it made you feel. By writing to my mentor I know he takes in what I write, and because of his advice I'm making my first B in an English class."

With their mentors' help, students who might have received Ds and Fs earned Cs and Bs. Students who would have gotten As and Bs in any case were intensely engaged in the personal issues that arose and in the opportunity to find out what kind of people are behind bars. All the writing mentors, especially those who were self-educated and had not enjoyed much recognition of their accomplishments, experienced increased self-esteem and increased confidence in their intellectual ability. Lyle, a prisoner who was not a writing mentor, wrote to tell Kendall about his friend Gilbert, who was one of the mentors:

> When I first met Gilbert, we were clerks in the parts room of the maintenance department. Gilbert has always seemed nice enough; he just struck me as wanting something to fill this huge void caused by his actions and guilt. If only you could have seen this guy when you wrote and told him he

was accepted as a writing mentor for college students! He beamed with pride as he shared his letter with us. Here was this guy feeling useless, hopeless. When you gave this man an opportunity to help you reach some students; when you put faith in him and told him he was worth something; when you placed him on your level, a normal human level, you ignited his heart and his brain and made him begin to grow again.

Prisoners weren't the only ones whose hearts and brains ignited in this process. Prima, a student for whom English is a third language, and who stated on the first day of class that she hated English, wrote in her evaluation, "When I was in high school I just wrote to fill up the pages and get it over with. I didn't care what I put down. The teachers didn't even read it. But the way my mentors connect with me tells me that what I'm saying matters. Somebody's listening. It's real different."

Writing mentors take a personal interest in their students; they remember what their students have revealed about themselves from one essay to the next, and they bring their own experiences into the dialogue. Isaac, who is serving forty years, wrote to one of his students,

James, I loved your essay. You have invited the reader to share in the intimate, infernal misery of a man whose only reason for living is that he has another drink to consume. Even if I wasn't aware of the strict upbringing of your father or the rigors you encountered as a soldier in Iraq, you still help me to understand that your need for dissolution was so pronounced that a turn down the path to alcoholism was perhaps inevitable. Your tale mirrors countless others, including mine. I thank you for sharing so personal a part of yourself when you could have easily chosen a topic less painful in the telling.

But students have to earn this kind of praise. A student named Ben tried to get away with recycling what must have been an old high school paper about the effects of spanking as a form of discipline. His paper was badly organized, impersonal, and vague. His mentor, Madeline, who Ben describes as "a hard-headed woman" wouldn't accept it. She responded,

> Ben, I'm still not sure what your position is on this issue. Should spankings be a last resort after all else has failed? Should there be a law against spankings? Do some kids need occasional spankings? You say, "Spankings may be harmful," but you provide the reader with no evidence, no details to support this claim. Give more details. You go on to say, "Spankings may alter the child's behavior," but you don't say how. These are just unsupported assumptions. Where's your critical thinking? Finally you claim, "Childhood spankings may result in future criminal behavior or mental instability." But where's your evidence? Do you have hospital/police reports? Do you have personal testimonies? You can't just make claims like these with nothing to back them up.

Kendall assigned students to write descriptive essays about people who have changed their lives, cause-and-effect essays examining decisions they have made, and essays in which they must define the term *criminal*. Each of these topics resulted in meaningful exchanges between students and mentors. For example, Gilbert wrote this to one of his students:

> I have always believed that the media stresses the negative in order to keep the public in fear and to help the government get what it wants. It's a form of control. The only way people out there in the free world will ever know the truth about prison is if those of us in prison share it from in here. I fight hard to never lose what little decency I came in here with. I want the world to see that not all inmates are as they are portrayed in the media. Some men in here just made a terrible mistake.

Matt, who would have done well in the course anyway, writes, "I feel like I'm getting an understanding of our judicial system from writing to my mentors. I never knew much about who goes to prison, or why they go there. Now I have an inside view." Other students care more about the fact that getting help from their mentors is helping them succeed, and their evaluations sound like advertising sound bites. Rehmat, a young woman who has only lived in the United States a few years, writes, "A teacher can help, but he/she has many students, and in this program it is like you have your own private teacher." Shea writes, "I have taken English 1301 before. We wrote the same number of papers in this class as in the other class, but this time I will pass, and possibly with a C, because of the input I got from the mentors." Margaret adds, "With just a teacher looking over the papers and making short comments, I wouldn't have gotten so much of a deep look at what I was doing."

Margaret is right. Her teachers' comments have never been so extensive as the comments she gets from her mentors. Length, however, is not always the key. Kenneth, who has spent much of his life behind bars and is a skilled writer of powerful short stories, writes pithy responses to his student, Jonathan, such as, "I just want you to stop using so many words to say something simple. I mean detail is OK, but you are trying to be too 'literary.' I think once I can get you to tone it down a little bit, then we will see your best work." Jonathan, in his evaluation of the program, writes,

> My mentors pointed out that I use too many words, and I often use words I don't really understand (thank you Mr. Thesaurus). I rewrote my first paper in normal English and received a 95 (thank you writing mentors)! My interaction with my writing mentors not only made me a better writer, it gave me perspective. After getting to know my mentors, I feel things are not as bad as I make them out to be, my life could be much worse, and I should make the most of the opportunity I have right now.

The development of perspective is a theme in many students' comments on the project. Jonathan learned to say what he means and to quit complaining about his life. Kenneth's other student, Ebony, writes, "Kenneth talks to me about relaxing while I write, something I never thought about before. I find it helps me to think clearly. In addition, Kenneth helped me to sympathize with my father, who is in jail. Until now, I didn't want anything to do with my father. So now I've decided to start writing my father."

The shifts in perspective are not all on the students' side. Lawrence, a mentor who was estranged from his daughters until recently, received an essay from a young woman about her father as "an absent hero" who deserted his family. Lawrence confided in Ashley,

> You write, "After all, my mother has reminded me for years of what a loser my father is and will always be; and he can never do anything correctly." That comment touched home for me. My daughters were told the same thing about me, and I cried when I read that. What I would like to know is, *how* was your father your hero? For example, you write, "When he left the household he did not look back." But you could say, "When he left the household he did not look back, my father who many a night saved me from my scary dreams." See what I did? I told the reader why or how he was my hero. I would like to know more about the ways you were like your father. I believe if you added more information there, you would allow the reader to see and feel your need to understand your father and the part of yourself that you feel is like him. Reading your essay made me an emotional wreck. You allowed me to see in words how I hurt my children through my selfishness.

One of the most effective coping strategies mentors demonstrate is a sense of humor. John F., who says he sports a "full body suit" of tattoos, writes to his student, "Go back to your textbook and read about critical thinking. You are confusing association with cause. A Texas adage comes to mind: 'Just 'cause you put them boots in the oven don't make 'em country biscuits.'"

Halfway through the semester Guadalupe, who taught himself to read and write in jail, attached a note with the response to his student, saying, "Doc, it's hard for me to write these responses for the simple fact that I ain't no better than these cats, and I feel like a hypocrite. I'm sure I can write a cause-and-effect essay myself now. I think writing these responses helped me to understand how to do it, but I do feel stupid. This stuff is a real challenge." His note was attached to a response that included classic English teachers' advice: "Shouldn't your introduction end with a thesis sentence?" Gently but persistently, he continues, "Then in the body, in my point of view, if you would have used more specific detail, your essay would have came out better."

Kendall felt personally understood and supported by many of the mentors' notes. John C. wrote, "I found these cause-and-effect essays a little harder to comment on than the descriptive essays, but I did my best. Two of the students didn't follow directions, and the third turned his in two days late. I must say that after this round I don't envy you much. I can understand how your job can be very rewarding, much like seeing a butterfly emerge from its cocoon. On the other hand I can also see why you have migraine headaches."

Often prisoners achieved significant insights as a result of thinking about their students' essays. Guillermo is in solitary confinement because he was once a gang member. He's self-educated, and he reads Thucydides and Lao Tzu and mentions their works in his responses. Guillermo spends twenty-three hours a day in a six-by-nine-foot cell. He wrote to his student,

> Craig, your paragraphs are neat and in order. The words and phrases smell of your military background. You and I have more in common than I initially thought. I also had a drinking problem when I was out there. I would get drunk and start fights. In fact I picked up these cases I'm down here for while I was on one of my binges. Next month makes thirteen years I've been down. What does this have to do with you? You describe the effects very clearly: 1) destroyed my marriage, 2) gave

me a dishonorable discharge from the Marines, and 3) made me distant from my family. It's real easy to say the cause was alcohol. I've done that. But there was something way deeper than just booze. I have this self-destructive mechanism buried in my subconscious, and this rage in my heart that would surface when I drank. I'm not saying this is the case for you, but I would suggest you look deeper into the cause of those effects. What's the root cause? It's just something to reflect on. The essay will stand as it is, but it could lead to something more important than an assignment for a class.

Many students experienced the "something more important" aspect of this work. Hilario, a nineteen-year-old student and father with a full-time job and a full-time course load, found that his mentors opened his eyes. He explained, "At the same time I was learning how to improve my papers, I was learning about the mentors' lives. We all make mistakes; some of us learn from them. The mentors want you to keep your head on straight, and they give you advice worth listening to." Kyle has dyslexia. He had three mentors who attended to every sentence in each of his papers. One of his mentors, Tom, told Kyle to try reading his papers aloud, carefully and slowly, so he would notice when he left words out of sentences or letters out of words. Kyle tried that system and got his first B in English.

Having teaching assistants who are eager to read and respond to students' work, and who have hours to focus on that work, restores to the business of education some of the heart and spirit the Romans had in mind when they coined the word educare, based on the Greek word meaning "to draw out." As writing mentor Jesse says, "You have to pull their own truth out of their minds." This drawing out from students takes us back to the medieval ideal of the university as a place where tutors and students engage in dialogue about content, even as they hone their skills in rhetoric.

How you might do something similar

Kendall devised the following process for setting up a writing mentor program. Inventive readers may find ways to simplify, adapt, or redesign these steps to suit their own situations.

Invite a pool of prisoners to participate. You may reach them via radio, a chaplain, or a notice posted in the prison with permission of the warden. If the prison has an educational program, the head of that program may be helpful. Be clear that this is not for pay and not for credit. You should also be wary of describing your mentoring project as an "educational program"; educational programs are often vetoed by wardens in Texas who feel that education is a privilege prisoners have to earn and that has to be paid for by their families. This is merely the exchange of letters between a private citizen who is a teacher and a prisoner or a group of prisoners. Prisoners should apply by writing the teacher a letter explaining why they would like to participate and what they have to offer. Set a deadline for this letter no more than two weeks after the announcement.

Use your work address or a post-office box for all correspondence. Use your own full name, but use only the first names of your students. Your students will receive only the first names of the prisoners. Neither students nor prisoners should contact each other directly. All mail goes through the teacher, and the teacher reads it all to be sure that 1) students do not reveal their full identities, home neighborhoods, or workplaces; 2) students do not assume superiority and begin to impose their religious, political, or other beliefs on their mentors (discussion of these issues can be fruitful, but some students have a tendency to think they can "save" their mentors); and 3) prisoners do not slip into seduction, requests for money or favors, requests that students contact them directly, or imposition of their beliefs on the students.

Screen the pool of potential mentors. Send respectfully written form letters to all those who express an interest in finding a romantic pen pal (probably about half your pool). Explain that this is not that kind of program. If you detect mental disturbance or requests for money or services in any letters, send respectfully written form letters saying you have received more applications than you have spaces for, thanks. Sift through the applications and select about twice as many as you think you can use.

Write to the potential mentors. Explain what your course is about, what your objectives are, and how you would like the mentors to work with you. Send a sample exercise (part of a student's paper, proposal, or assignment) and invite the potential mentors to respond to it. Give them guidelines so they know how to respond helpfully. Give them a deadline for sending their responses to you, no more than two weeks after the date of your letter. Be sure to explain that you have more applicants than spaces, and you will make your decisions based on these responses.

Evaluate your results and choose your mentors. Many prisoners are self-educated. Prisoners' formal education does not necessarily indicate their ability to mentor college students. Kendall found it helpful, but not necessary, to assign two mentors per student, so each student has more than one response to the work. Some mentors can handle up to five or six students. All mentors should have at least two students, so they have some basis of comparison.

Write two letters. One letter should gently explain that you had to make some difficult choices, and unfortunately the applicants receiving the letter were not selected for the program. The second letter should thank the mentors you have chosen, give them a time-line for when to expect work from students and when to send their responses back to you. Provide them photocopied reading mate-rial that may be helpful to them in offering feedback to students and ask them to write a two-page introduction of themselves for their students.

Most states will not allow individuals to send books directly to prisoners; they may have to be sent by the publisher or a retailer. More information about this will probably be on the website for your state's prison system.

Inform your students. Kendall found it useful to make the Writing Mentor Program optional for students in her class, but also to explain the program in such a way that its attractiveness and usefulness to the student are apparent. She only had one student out of more than a hundred in two semesters who did not want to participate. That student's father had been killed by a carjacker. Those students who participate submit three copies of their work: one to keep on file, and one to each mentor. Students identify themselves on the papers by first name only. If two students have the same first name, one may choose to use a middle name. A teacher doing this on a larger scale might want to have students use their first name and the first initial of their last name.

Assign students to mentors. Depending on the size of the student pool and the mentor pool, it may be possible to distribute prisoners' introductions and let students choose their mentors on the basis of those introductions. If the groups are very large (as in Kendall's case—twenty-six mentors and fifty-two students per semester), simply make the decisions yourself and keep a log. Kendall used a class roll sheet, and by each student's name she wrote the names of the mentors assigned to the student. Then she asked students to write two-page introductions of themselves to send to their mentors.

Get clerical assistance, if possible. This program requires significant administrative work, including addressing envelopes, sorting the students' work and putting it into envelopes going to the prisoners, distributing copies of introductions, weighing each package of materials, affixing postage, and mailing. A teacher who has a paid student assistant or teaching assistant could delegate these chores.

Plan the timetable carefully. You will have learned from your preliminary work how long it takes mail to travel between the prison(s) and back. Students will need to turn in their work, wait while their mentors respond, receive their work back, and revise it.

Students often choose to write letters to their mentors discussing the mentors' responses. Allow at least several weeks for these exchanges to take place.

Some students establish meaningful relationships with their mentors and want to continue the correspondence. Kendall decided that at the end of the course, after the work is finished and grades are in, if a student obtains a post-office box, Kendall would make the prisoner's full address information available. But there should never be an expectation on the part of the student or the prisoner that their relationship will continue after the class ends.

Buckle your seatbelt. Kendall was often moved to tears, to laughter, and to deep reflection by the exchanges between prisoners and students. Their work was profound. Sometimes she felt a bit voyeuristic, but by making it clear to students and prisoners from the beginning that she would be reading all correspondence, she was at least a *visible* voyeur. Honesty, clarity, and respect for all participants are key.

What Prisoners Can Teach Us

AT THE THOREAU CONGREGATION we have tried to design programs that challenge a common assumption underlying many prison ministries: that people on the outside will bring the gifts of time, insight, maturity, and stability to needy prisoners. We have tried to challenge the notion that the gift of "salvation" works only in one direction. We have been humbled and delighted by the gifts of insight and compassion we have received from prisoners. They have taught us some important lessons through our work together. Kendall assembled some of these teachings in a short essay, which is the basis for these concluding remarks.

Prisoners teach us strength. They teach us that it is possible to live in the blast furnace of a Texas summer, shoved into cages with hundreds of other beings in vast metal shacks without air conditioning, and maintain not merely humanity but even (in some cases) grace, generosity, and kindness. They teach us that it is possible to live with inadequate medical attention, or none at all, while battling HIV/AIDS, hepatitis C, diabetes, cancer, heart failure, epilepsy, fractured bones, open wounds, skin disease, bipolar disorder, and every other disorder, named or unnamed, of mind and body.

Prisoners teach us courage. They show us that it is possible to live unflinchingly with daily physical and mental abuse, with the ever-present possibility of meeting violent death, with invasive body searches, with verbal attacks from guards and other prisoners, and with institutional indifference, negligence, and hostility. Prisoners teach us the courage of taking a heart full of hope before an indifferent, overworked parole board. They teach us that we could be separated from our children, our family, and all those we love, and still go on living.

Prisoners demonstrate how we would live if we had been caught and held accountable for the many infractions of law or custom we have violated and gotten away with. They show us the range of choices that would lie before us if our possessions, distractions, relationships, and addictions were stripped away, if our identities were reduced to numbers, if our illusions about ourselves were torn away like underwear, if we were labeled guilty, if we were regarded as embarrassments to our families and disappointments to our children, left to stew in our shame. Prisoners teach us to wonder who we would be in those circumstances, and to examine who we are now, endowed with the privilege of witnessing their world but free to leave when we like.

Prisoners teach us new dimensions of what we already know: that every human being has fundamental worth, each of us completely different from every other; and that we all have the capacity for violence, greed, selfishness, compassion, generosity, and empathy. In their lives we see our lives, and when we measure our accomplishments against theirs, given the differences in our circumstances, the comparison often does not flatter us.

Prisoners teach us transcendence. When they write to us about their childhoods, their passions, and their failings, we feel our commonality. When they meet us and lower the masks of indifference they wear for survival, we feel honored. When they mourn their losses in our presence and consider what to do with what is left for them, they teach us humility. When we meet face to face and they greet us with humor and gratitude, we know they have leapt hurdles we have never had to confront.

Not all prisoners are able to teach these lessons. There are many who cannot read or write and don't, therefore, correspond with anyone. There are some who are so wounded that they have become the wound itself, rotten and festering. There are some who distrust all outsiders, who fill their time with schemes and fantasies we would not want to know about, who have no desire to know us or any other free-world squares who might come their way.

Those of us at Thoreau involved in prison work know the prisoners who seek us out—those who write letters, who listen to *The Prison Show* and volunteer to help college students, who show up for a noncredit creative-writing workshop and support one another as they confront their demons and examine and describe their lives. If they are writing to us, studying with us, or talking with us, they have overcome doubts about our motives; they have made judgments about what it is safe to share. Not all prisoners have achieved transcendence and not all can teach us how to transcend our own obstacles. But the ones we know are sailing over barriers that would knock us flat. They teach us things we need to know to become better people.

UUA 2005 Statement of Conscience: Criminal Justice and Prison Reform

Background

This Statement of Conscience of the Unitarian Universalist Association builds upon more than a dozen social witness statements on criminal justice adopted by the Unitarian Universalist Association between 1961 and 2002. In June 2003, the General Assembly of the UUA selected "Criminal Justice and Prison Reform" as the issue suggested to congregations for two years of study, action, and reflection. The Commission on Social Witness (CSW) received initial reports from congregations and districts in March 2004. In June 2004, the CSW held a workshop on this issue at the General Assembly. An initial draft Statement of Conscience was distributed to all congregations and districts for their reflection and feedback in October 2004. At its March 2005 meeting, the CSW prepared a revised draft that was included in the final agenda book for the June 2005 General Assembly. A mini-assembly was held on Friday, June 24, at 8:00 A.M., to receive proposed amendments. The CSW met later in the day to consider all amendments and to prepare the revised draft Statement of Conscience that was debated by the General Assembly during its Saturday morning plenary, and then received the two-thirds vote required for adoption. There is an Addendum to this Statement of Conscience that provides additional background on these issues. Further information and the texts of other UUA Statements of Conscience can be found at the CSW website (www.uua.org/csw).

As Unitarian Universalists, we are committed to affirming the inherent goodness and worth of each of us. As Americans, we take pride in our constitutional promise of liberty, equality, and justice for all, including those who have violated the law. Yet the incarceration rate in the United States is five- to tenfold that of other nations, even those without such a constitutional promise. Our corrections system is increasingly rife with inequitable sentencing, longer terms of detention, racial and ethnic profiling, and deplorable jail and prison conditions and treatment. The magnitude of injustice and inequity in this system stands in stark contrast to the values that our nation—and our faith—proclaim. We are compelled to witness this dissonance between what America proclaims for criminal justice and what America practices. We offer an alternative moral vision of a justice system that operates in harmonious accord with our values as a community of faith. This vision includes the presumption of innocence, fair judicial proceedings, the merciful restoration of those who have broken the law, the renunciation of torture and other abusive practices, and a fundamental commitment to the dignity and humane treatment of everyone in our society, including prisoners.

The Current Crisis

In 2004, the United States incarcerated 2.2 million people in its prisons and jails. Among industrialized nations, the United States incarcerates the largest percentage of its population. There are also stark disparities in the racial composition of our nation's prisons, as African Americans account for fully half of the prison population and comprise only thirteen percent of the total population. Costs of imprisonment have increased due to state legislatures criminalizing an increasing number of activities, mandatory incarceration, and mandatory minimum sentencing. In response to these increased costs as well as lobbying by industry groups, state legislatures have increasingly privatized prisons, introducing profitability into the already conflicted structure of prison funding. Post-9/11 public fears have intensified the perceived need for retributive policies and have undermined those that are redemptive, rehabilitative, and restorative. Elected leaders and their constituents commonly conspire in this politics of fear.

Although Americans take great pride in the freedoms we espouse, the American prison system violates basic human rights in many ways. The Universal Declaration of Human Rights, which the United States endorsed in 1948, states in Article 5, "No one shall be subjected to torture or to cruel, inhuman, or degrading treatment or punishment." American correctional practice often subjects inmates to abusive treatment, such as torture and rape, and neglects basic human needs such as health care and nutrition. Some suspects are detained without charge, legal counsel, or access to family. While indigent defendants have exactly the same rights to competent counsel as non-indigent defendants, in many states indigent defendants are not provided equality of representation.

The American penchant for retribution squanders opportunities for redemption, rehabilitation, and restoration of the individual offender. Failures in the criminal justice system have created a disenfranchised, stigmatized class who are predominantly from lower-income backgrounds, poorly educated, or from racial and ethnic minorities. The punishment for crime is often simply separation from society, and the sentence one serves *is* the punishment. In our penal system, punishment often continues even after those convicted have completed their sentence. They are often stripped of voting rights, denied social services, and barred from many professions. If convicted of a drug crime, they become ineligible for federal student loans to attend college. Our criminal justice system makes it exceedingly difficult for anyone to reintegrate into society. People returning to their communities find that they lack opportunity, skills, and social services to fully function in society and hold down jobs, maintain families, or participate in their communities. Therefore, an unacceptable percentage of those released from our prisons and jails recidivate.

Not all prisoners who enter the system leave. One of the most shameful aspects of our current criminal justice system is the death penalty. Many countries have abandoned the practice of capital punishment. Studies fail to demonstrate that the death penalty actually deters crime. While the United States Supreme Court has ruled against the execution of juvenile offenders, the death penalty is still legal in the United States. Experience shows that judges and juries wrongly convict defendants. Given the number of death row inmates released on account of innocence, it is highly likely that we have executed innocent people and will do so again in the future unless we abolish the death penalty.

Toward a New Corrections Philosophy

The first two Principles of Unitarian Universalism address the inherent worth and dignity of every person and justice, equity, and compassion in human relations. Consistent with these fundamental principles, a new corrections policy must place a primary emphasis on community alternatives.

Community alternatives should be developed in the context of redemptive, rehabilitative, and restorative justice. Redemptive justice recognizes justice as relational. Its purpose is to restore wholeness and rightness in the social order and in the disposition of the offender, not to exact revenge. Rehabilitative justice is a process of education, socialization, and empowerment of the person to the status whereby she or he may be able to contribute constructively and appreciably to society. Restorative justice is a process whereby the offender can reconcile with the victim through appropriate restitution, community service, and healing measures.

A greatly expanded emphasis on community alternatives will provide substantial cost savings. These savings may and should be in community support services such as literacy education, vocational training, drug addiction treatment, viable employment, and affordable housing. The benefits of these services are in the quality of life for the offending person, the victim, the families of the offender and victim, and the increased safety and security of the community.

Separation from society may well be appropriate punishment for many crimes, but society's responsibility does not end there. A corrections system driven by compassionate justice would prepare offenders for successful reentry into society. An overwhelming majority of those who are incarcerated return to their communities, yet only a small percentage receive meaningful rehabilitative programming while in prison. In the reformed system, they will receive substantial rehabilitative services, including mental health treatment, educational programs, and vocational training during incarceration and employment and transitional housing once released. Redemption, rehabilitation, and restoration are not only humanely forgiving of those who have fallen off the main societal track; they are more effective and less costly in addressing the criminal justice needs of our whole society.

A Call to Unitarian Universalists

Appalled by the gross injustices in our current criminal justice system, we the member congregations of the Unitarian Universalist Association commit ourselves to working in our communities to reform the criminal justice and correctional systems and effect justice for both victims and violators. We act in the spirit that we are indeed our sisters' and our brothers' keepers. Love is our governing principle in all human relationships. Therefore, that we may speak with one voice in unity, though not uniformity, we commit ourselves, our congregations, and our Association to these congregational actions and advocacy goals.

Congregational Actions

- Form a study group within the congregation to learn about the local jail and state prison system, its budget, recidivism rates, rehabilitation programs (inside and outside the facilities), and opportunities for volunteers.

- Network and collaborate with existing community outreach programs and advocacy groups for prisoners and their families.
- Establish Unitarian Universalist prison ministries and encourage volunteers from the congregation to go into prisons and get involved with and/or begin peer-counseling and mentoring programs.
- Address reentry issues by engaging in supportive work with formerly incarcerated individuals to reduce recidivism and increase success in the probation and parole system.
- Reach out and support congregational members who are personally affected by the criminal justice system.

Advocacy Goals

- Legislation that strengthens gun control, ends the so-called War on Drugs, disallows mandatory minimum sentencing, provides for fair, equitable, anti-racist sentencing , and abolishes the death penalty.
- Reforms of the judicial system to establish drug courts that prescribe treatment rather than imprisonment, provide affordable and competent counsel for all defendants, and empower citizen review boards.
- Effective alternatives to incarceration such as arbitration, restorative justice programs, community service, in-house arrest, and mental health and substance abuse treatment.
- Dismantling of the for-profit prison industry.
- A publicly funded and managed system of correctional facilities accredited by the National Commission on Correctional Health Care and by the American Correctional Association, ensuring that children and

youth in custody are separated from adults in the penal system, providing appropriate facilities and services for prisoners with mental health and other health concerns, addressing the unique medical and psychological needs of female prisoners, stopping prisoner rape, and abolishing cruel detention and interrogation methods and the use of isolation for prolonged periods of time.

- Termination of the relocation of prisoners out of state or out of country.
- Support for families and family life by assigning prisoners to facilities near their homes, by providing facilities that are conducive to comfortable family visits, by maintaining parental rights as appropriate, and by allowing prison mothers to raise their infants.
- Universal access to rehabilitation, education, and job training programs and restorative and recovery programs for non-religious as well as for religious prisoners.
- A probation and parole system empowered and enabled to correct the excesses of past mandatory sentencing requirements, provide compassionate reprieves for the terminally ill and aged, support former prisoners as they reenter society, and allow for individual evaluation of technical parole violations.
- Elimination of post-prison restrictions on civil rights and civil liberties, including voting rights.

Through ongoing congregational education, advocacy, and action, we can make good on our Unitarian Universalist heritage and our American promise to be both compassionate and just to all in our society. Through our diligence and perseverance in realizing this promise, we can live the core values of our country and extend the values of our faith to the benefit of others.

Resources

Literature by prisoners and about prison writing

Abbot, Jack Henry. *In the Belly of the Beast: Letters from Prison.* Introduction by Norman Mailer. New York: Vintage Books, 1981.

AIDS Counseling and Education Program of the Bedford Hills Correctional Facility. *Breaking the Walls of Silence: AIDS and Women in a New York State Maximum-Security Prison.* Forewords by Whoopi Goldberg and Elaine A. Lord, superintendent. Woodstock, NY: Overlook Press, 1998.

Baca, Jimmy Santiago. *A Place to Stand: The Making of a Poet.* New York: Grove Press, 2001.

Bridge Foundation, ed. *Fighting the Demons: An Anthology of Poetry and Drawings Connected with Prison, by Prisoners, Family Members, and Other Connected People.* Charnwood, Australia: Ginninderra Press, 2004.

Chevigny, Bell Gale, ed. *Doing Time: 25 Years of Prison Writing.* Foreword by Sister Helen Prejean. New York: Arcade Publishing, 1999.

Ehrman, Donald, Jr. *From the Inside Out: A Book of Poetry Written on the Inside to Be Read on the Outside*. Orange, CA: Ehrman Entertainment, 1996.

Evans, Jeff, ed. *Undoing Time: American Prisoners in Their Own Words*. Foreword by Jimmy Santiago Baca. Boston: Northeastern University Press, 2001.

Franklin, H. Bruce, ed. *Prison Writing in Twentieth-Century America*. Foreword by Tom Wicker. New York: Penguin Books, 1998.

Harris, Jean. *"They Always Call Us Ladies": Stories from Prison*. New York: Scribner, 1988.

Lerner, Jimmy A. *You Got Nothing Coming: Notes from a Prison Fish*. New York: Broadway Books, 2002.

Lippert, Phillip. *God Bless America: Stories by Some Guy in the Joint*. Adrian, MI: Phillip Lippert Defense Fund, 2000.

Martin, Dannie M., and Peter Y. Sussman. *Committing Journalism: The Prison Writings of Red Hog*. New York: Norton, 1995.

Masters, Jarvis Jay. *Finding Freedom: Writings from Death Row*. Junction City, CA: Padma Publishing, 1997.

Middleton, Patrick. *Healing Our Imprisoned Minds: A People's Guide to Hope and Freedom*. West Conshohocken, PA: Infinity Publishing Company, 2004.

Morgan, Seth, and Edward Posada, eds. *About Time: An Anthology of California Prison Writing*. Santa Cruz, CA: Vacaville Prison Literary Workshop Program, 1980.

Raúlrsalinas. *Un Trip Through the Mind Jail y Otras Excursions*. Houston: Arte Publico Press, 1999.

Raúlsalinas. *Raúlsalinas and the Jail Machine: My Weapon Is My Pen: Selected Writings by Raúl Salinas*. Austin: University of Texas Press, 2006.

Scheffler, Judith A., ed. *Wall Tappings: An International Anthology of Women's Prison Writings, 200 to the Present.* 2nd ed. New York: Feminist Press, 2002.

Shelton, Richard, and Ken Lamberton, eds. *Walking Rain Review.* Tucson, AZ: Post Litho Printing, 1989–2008. Journal of original writing by prisoners.

Literature about prison life and working with prisoners

Bosworth, Mary, ed. *The Encyclopedia of Prisons and Correctional Facilities.* Thousand Oaks, CA: Sage Publications, 2005.

Gordon, Robert Ellis, and inmates of the Washington Corrections System. *The Funhouse Mirror: Reflections on Prison.* Pullman, WA: Washington State University Press, 2000.

Hulme, Chris. *Manslaughter United: A Season with a Prison Football Team.* London: Yellow Jersey Press, 1999.

Jensen, Derrick. *Walking on Water: Reading, Writing, and Revolution.* White River Junction, VT: Chelsea Green Publishing, 2004.

Lamb, Wally, ed., with the women of Niantic Correctional Institution. *Couldn't Keep It to Myself: Testimonies from Our Imprisoned Sisters.* New York: Regan Books, 2003.

Leder, Drew, with inmates of the Maryland Penitentiary. *The Soul Knows No Bars: Inmates Reflect on Life, Death, and Hope.* New York: Rowman & Littlefield, 2000.

Lozoff, Bo. *It's a Meaningful Life: It Just Takes Practice.* New York: Penguin Compass, 2000.

Lozoff, Bo. *We're All Doing Time.* Durham, NC: Human Kindness Foundation, 1985.

"Prison." *Parabola* 28 (May 2003). Includes articles, fiction, poetry, and art on the subject of prisons and people in prisons.

Salzman, Mark. *True Notebooks*. New York: Knopf, 2003.

Stoodley, Sheryl, ed. *The World Split Open: Theatre and Writing by Women in Prison*. Afterword by K. Kendall. Northampton, MA: Cultural Images Group, 1989.

Tannenbaum, Judith. *Disguised as a Poem: My Years Teaching Poetry at San Quentin*. Boston: Northeastern University Press, 2000.

Thompson, Leon "Whitey." *Rock Hard: The Autobiography of a Former Alcatraz Inmate*. New York: Pocket Books, 1994.

Trustone, Judith, et al. *Celling America's Soul: Torture and Transformation in Our Prisons*. Haverford, PA: Infinity Publishing, 2003.

Whitney, Kobai Scott. *Sitting Inside; Buddhist Practice in America's Prisons*. Boulder: Prison Dharma Network, 2003.

Wideman, John Edgar. *Brothers and Keepers*. New York: Holt, Rinehart and Winston, 1984.

Internet Resources

Facts and statistics about prisons and the prison industry

www.anarchistblackcross.org
   The Anarchist Black Cross Network advocates for prisoners, supports political action on behalf of prisoners, and provides information about the prison industry. It also sponsors local groups involved in this work.

www.justicepolicy.org
> The Justice Policy Institute generates research on society's reliance on incarceration, alternative sentencing, prison conditions, and much more.

www.prisonsucks.com
> Research on prisons including statistics, book reviews, fact sheets, articles, and up-to-date links to information of interest to people who work with or support the rights of prisoners.

www.realcostofprisons.org
> Background papers, workshop materials, news and recent research updates, and information about the prison industry. An activity of the Sentencing Project, a Washington DC-based nonprofit organization dedicated to reducing over-reliance on incarceration.

www.sentencingproject.org
> The Sentencing Project is one of the nation's leading organizations that develops alternative sentencing programs, conducts policy research on U.S. criminal justice, and advocates for creating meaningful reforms.

www.tcadp.org
> Texas Coalition to Abolish the Death Penalty. News lists, e-mail lists, and suggestions for action.

Prisoners, education and the arts

www.azstarnet.com/sn/110degrees/23826.php
> "Writing Beyond Bars," by Reyna Padilla. June 2004 *Arizona Daily Star* article about the work of Richard Shelton, founder of Arizona state prison writing workshops.

www.communityarts.net
> The Community Arts Network is a Web portal with a section devoted to Arts in Corrections.

www.friendsjournal.org/contents/2002/10october/feature.html
Stephen Angell, a founder of the Quaker Alternatives to Violence Project, which offers workshops on nonviolence in prisons and elsewhere, is interviewed in this online article in *Friends Journal.*

www.judithtannenbaum.com
Resources related to Judith Tannenbaum's extensive experience with prison workshops in California.

www.kenmentor.com/papers/corrections_ed.htm
"Corrections Education" is an excellent article by Kenneth Mentor about the value of prison education.

www.lairdcarlson.com
The Cell Door is an Internet zine written by prisoners and their families and friends for people in the free world. It includes links to petitions to support prisoners and to endorse prison reforms.

www.lostvault.com
LostVault is a website containing thousands of postings by prisoners seeking pen pals. Unlike several other pen pal sites, LostVault does not charge a fee for listings. It includes an active discussion board for exploring issues related to corresponding with prisoners.

www.lsa.umich.edu/English/pcap/index.html
The Prison Creative Arts Project at the University of Michigan has an 18-year history of facilitating workshops and arts programs in prisons and of mentoring prisoners upon their release.

www.pen.org
The PEN Awards honor the best writing by prisoners each year. The website also includes ordering information for a handbook for prison writers and a handbook for starting a writing workshop in prison.

www.spoonjackson.com
Website of California prison poet Spoon Jackson.

www.thirdworldtraveler.com/Prison_System/Masked_Racism_ADavis.html
Essay by Angela Davis, "Masked Racism: Reflections on the Prison Industrial Complex."

http://web.grinnell.edu/groups/prison/index.html
This website showcases a student-run program at Grinnell University that provides prisoners with a liberal arts education.

Prisoners and spirituality

www.prison.dhamma.org
Vipassana meditation courses are taught in prisons in India, the United States, and Canada. This site describes the courses and features guidelines for those who would like to set up courses in additional locations.

www.humankindness.org
This website includes the Prison-Ashram Project, a Buddhist-based meditation and substance abuse treatment program that has been operating since 1973, directed by Bo and Sita Lozoff.

www.engaged-zen.org
Website of the Engaged Zen Foundation, an independent organization with headquarters in Maine, originally founded to foster zazen (seated contemplative meditation) practice in prison. The website features articles, talks, and links to sources of information about prisons, the death penalty, and conscientious objector status.

www.pfi.org
"The mission of Prison Fellowship is to mobilize and assist the Christian community in its ministry to prisoners, ex-prisoners, victims, and their families; and in the advancement of restorative justice."

Prisoners and their families and friends

www.tifa.org

> The mission of the Texas Inmate Families Association is to help break the cycle of crime by strengthening families through support, education, and advocacy. Includes links to legislative information, actions, and more.

Acknowledgments

The projects described in this book were supported financially and spiritually by the Henry David Thoreau Unitarian Universalist Congregation in Stafford, Texas. Without the careful guidance of Rev. Bill Clark, our minister when we began these projects, and Rev. Paul Beedle, our minister as we continue them; without the participation of many committed members of our congregation; and without the support of Thoreau's social action committee, led by Sue Ann Lorig, none of this would have happened.

Inspiration has come from many powerful writers who found their voices in prison and from prisoners who have become involved with our programs. I offer a deep bow of gratitude to Jimmy Santiago Baca and Jarvis Jay Masters. I urge anyone who is interested in the meaning of freedom to read their works. Other teachers known to me only through writings and film include free-world people who have built community with prisoners and shared some of their skills and secrets, including Sister Helen Prejean, Eve Ensler, Robert Gordon, Bo and Sita Lozoff, Judith Tannenbaum, Grady Hillman, Richard Shelton, and Quincy Troupe.

Family and friends have endured my absence of mind and body as Kendall and I were swept away by the power of this work, and I especially thank my children, Nia and Dash Speer, and Kendall's daughter, Manko Kendall, as well as my mother, Mary Speer, who assisted with child care on Monday evenings for nearly two years.

Deepest and most profound thanks go to the Texas prisoners with whom members of the Thoreau Congregation have created such an uncommon community. Many are mentioned in this book only by first names, and most are still incarcerated. They have embraced us "squares," without enough street sense to make it twenty-four hours in the neighborhoods where many of them grew up, "fish" privileged to come and go through steel gates that close on a world where the codes and dangers mystify, intrigue, and sometimes frighten. Many of the prisoners we have been privileged to meet through these projects have become our friends and our spiritual community. They have trusted us, grown with us, allowed us to love them, told us their secrets, and put up with our wide-eyed awe at learning about their life experiences and our admiration for their will to grow and change while enduring horrible circumstances. This little book is a small offering for them, and for the over two million people who live in cages in the most prosperous and powerful country in the world.